ARE THORESEN w
A doctor of veterinary
anthroposophic medi
puncture, osteopathy a~   ~~ 1981
he has run a private holi~ ~ practice in Sandefjord,
Norway, for the healing of small animals and
horses, as well as people. He has lectured widely, specializing in veterinary
acupuncture, and has published dozens of scholarly articles. In 1984 he
started to treat cancer patients, both human and animals, and this work has
been the focus of much of his recent research. He is the author of *Demons
and Healing* and several other books on complementary medicine published in various languages.

Experiences From the Threshold and Beyond

Understood Through Anthroposophy

Are Simeon Thoresen, DVM

TEMPLE LODGE

Temple Lodge Publishing Ltd.
Hillside House, The Square
Forest Row, RH18 5ES

www.templelodge.com

Published in English by Temple Lodge in 2019

Originally self-published in an earlier version under the title *Experiences from the Threshold—and beyond: Understood through Anthroposophy* via CreateSpace in 2019

© Are Simeon Thoresen, DVM

This new edition has been re-edited and expanded by Temple Lodge Publishing in cooperation with the author. With thanks to Michael Allen for his editorial contribution

A CIP catalogue record for this book is available from the British Library

ISBN 978 1 912230 33 4

Cover by Morgan Creative incorporating artwork © Kokotewan
Typeset by DP Photosetting, Neath, West Glamorgan
Printed and bound by 4Edge Ltd., Essex

Dedicated to all who seek to heal and understand

Contents

Foreword

This book aims to give readers an understanding of the *spiritual* foundations of the threshold, especially the practical experiences.

All my books are inspired either by the spiritual world or by experiences in front of, on, or beyond the threshold to the spiritual world.

The above may already confuse the average reader: What is the 'spiritual world'? What is the 'threshold'? What does 'passing the threshold' mean? What light can my life experiences throw upon such questions?

What's more, who was Rudolf Steiner? Does the 100 years that has passed since Rudolf Steiner's death make any difference to the answers to these questions?

Readers who are familiar with the concepts mentioned above will understand what I am trying to communicate, but others will have difficulties. As these questions will define this whole book, I will say a few words here on these subjects so that more readers will be able to comprehend them.

There is a physical world, which we all accept as real, but there is also a spiritual world, which interpenetrates this material world and which also is its cause and foundation.

Between these two worlds, a threshold exists that can be felt, seen clairvoyantly, traversed and passed through by anyone with a real desire to do so, after adequate training and sufficient time. At this threshold there is a guardian, whose task is to stop humans from passing across it unprepared, for then they might be seriously disturbed or frightened, as reality is so different on the other side of this spiritual border.

Later, in the Introduction, I will try to define these concepts further, but if already the reader feels uncomfortable with the themes and goals of this book, it might be better to put it down now.

Allow me then to continue. It is important to be aware that there are many thresholds in the spiritual world, many aspects of the 'Guardians of the Threshold', many versions of the so-called 'animals on the threshold' and many types of deaths when passing the different thresholds, as something is always lost or dies in such a passing. Also, the worlds beyond have a variety of different constructions, although they may appear the same for two spiritual researchers who enter the same 'room'. There are many rooms in the higher dimensions.[*]

---

[*] 'My Father's house has many rooms' (John 14:2).

Here we touch upon some very difficult concepts and expressions that will be defined and explained in the Introduction following this Foreword.

All of my earlier books, apart from *Demons and Healing*,[*] are self-published on Amazon and are each about a specific type of threshold crossing and a specific part of the world beyond.

- *Poplar* is about the spiritual experiences I had in nature, especially with trees, leading back to early childhood.
- *7-fold Way to Therapy* is about the spiritual experiences I had in developing my therapeutic methods, especially in relation to Rudolf Steiner's so-called 'First Class' of the School of Spiritual Science.
- *The Forgotten Mysteries of Atlantis* is about the spiritual experiences I had in understanding my personal karma, especially relating to my work.
- *Alternative Veterinary Medicine* is about the spiritual experiences I had as a veterinarian, trying to find my way from the materialistic medicine of today and towards a more spiritual practice.
- *Demons and Healing* is about the spiritual experiences I had in meeting the demonic structures causing disease and misfortune.
- *Spiritual Medicine* is about the spiritual experiences I had, resulting in the later development of my therapeutic methods, especially in finding the Christ force that resides in the middle (of everything), and also in understanding the huge danger and illusionary scam that 5-element acupuncture (Traditional Chinese medicine) has led us into.

So, if I have written about these themes all my life, why then another book about the same? The answer is simple. The books I have written previously are about the lessons, knowledge and inspirations I have received from the spirit. This book is about the *methods*, the *experiences* on the thresholds and the *techniques* I have used to enter the spiritual world. In other words, it is about how to approach the threshold, how to pass it and how to behave beyond it.

Rudolf Steiner and other authors have already written about this subject, but my own experiences are somewhat different from that of others, so I have decided to give an in-depth description of them: how I got there, how I behaved in the spiritual world and what mistakes I made. As I do this, I do not mean to criticize or correct any other writer, but just want to give my own experiences concerning the path described in this book.

[*] *Demons and Healing*, Temple Lodge Publishing 2018.

It is very important in connection with these examples to be aware of one of the most important laws of the spiritual world that the Greek philosopher Heraclitus[*] discovered: the law of non-repetition. This means that no experience on the threshold or beyond in the spiritual world will or can repeat itself. Every time I pass the threshold, I see different things, have different experiences and understand different concepts or truths of the spiritual realm of existence.

However, none of these experiences or revelations contradict each other. Therefore, not everyone who reads this book will experience the same as I describe here. I will only give examples of what can or may be experienced and a description of the many ways to enter the spiritual world and to pass the threshold.

★

In my opinion, we have but one possibility to save our culture, and that is to understand and accept that there is a spiritual world. If not, we will destroy ourselves in materialism. The only way to really 'believe' in a spiritual world is to experience it for ourselves, which an increasing amount of people want to do.

To do this we need to become more sensitive. Today, much attention is focused on those few with hypersensitivity towards the excesses of the material world, especially electromagnetic radiation and artificial additives. There are also hypersensitive children.

What today we need to become aware of is the opposite: the tragic *hypo*sensitivity towards the spiritual world, etheric radiation and spiritual beings. Without becoming more sensitive to these, we will be unable to 'see' all the destructiveness towards life we experience in the world today. And the only way to experience this world is to open our spiritual sense organs and pass the threshold.

In order to achieve this, there are two things that we must do:

- open or develop one or more of our spiritual organs of perception;
- pass the threshold by separating something in our soul (to be described later).

---

[*] Heraclitus (535–475 BCE) was a pre-Socratic Greek philosopher, famous for his insistence on ever-present change as being the fundamental essence of the universe, as stated in the famous saying, 'No man ever steps in the same river twice.' This is commonly considered to be one of the first digressions into the philosophical concept of becoming, and has been contrasted with Parmenides' statement that 'what is—is' as one of the first digressions into the philosophical concept of being.

The training necessary for opening the spiritual sense organs, with the resulting passing of the threshold, will be left for the last section of the book.

I have described my personal way over the threshold in the first four chapters:

- Childhood (6–12).
- Youth (12–21).
- Adulthood (21–62).
- Senior Years (62–).

This is because in these parts of my life it has been distinctly different as to how deep I could penetrate into the spiritual world, and therefore I will discuss them separately.

We will also see that in my early experiences, I only 'saw' things as imaginative pictures,* whether it was spiritual beings like elementals, the network between trees, or travelling in time and space. Later in life, these experiences have come back as 'understanding' brought about by working with the spiritual world. Rudolf Steiner describes this understanding as Inspiration.

In the latest part of my life, these 'understandings' seem to change the very structure or web of my brain, so that I feel myself to be inside the spiritual reality of which, initially, I was just a spectator through experiencing them as Imaginations, and later Inspirations. This last stage—of 'being inside' or living with the spiritual reality—Rudolf Steiner calls Intuition.

A good example of this development from Imagination via Inspiration to Intuition came about through the very complicated and challenging change of the curative effect of my cancer treatment. This treatment worked very well for 30 years (June 1984–March 2014), then stopped working completely for 4 years (March 2014–March 2018), only then to work again from March 2018 to the present. This will be an interesting example for learning for the reader, which I will explain in more detail in Chapter 4 of this book.†

---

* What Rudolf Steiner refers to as 'Imagination'.

† Whatever might be atavistic in my past or present spiritual abilities is not so relevant. What counts is the way we are conscious of what we are doing in the spiritual world and how morally responsible we are. We have all brought from past lives special faculties developed in different spiritual schools. Our natural clairvoyance is therefore very personal and individually developed. Rudolf Steiner's description of clairvoyant development and research is therefore not the model nor the standard to judge the other forms. All these different forms will metamorphose in the course of time.

With this example, we will also touch upon a very important fact concerning the passing of the threshold, the world beyond this threshold and also the training and exercises that must be done in order to go forward on this described path.

All efforts and training, even the slightest progress on the spiritual path, will be in vain if the motive is to further our own progress and knowledge of the spiritual world, or if we are driven by vanity. At this point in the book, it is very important to know this.

The only valid and fruitful reason for embarking on such a voyage is a wish to serve God and humanity, in any way, in the name of love on this long and painful path to spirituality. If we embark on this journey because we just want to know, to understand and to grow, it would be better if we didn't do it.

The words 'not I, but Christ in me' must be the only direction on this life-long path. If we do all this work for ourselves, the anguished words on the next page will come true. If we do it for the world, we might stand a chance.

Of Utmost Importance

Today, knowledge and insight of the spiritual world is vanishing rapidly, as materialism and egoism take their hold. Fewer and fewer people believe in God. Respect for other life forms, trees and animals, as well as for non-material beings, has lessened, and egoistic materialism is progressing. The culture is trembling under the weight of ignorance, and hyposensitivity. From where I stand, I cannot see any rescue or salvation.

Our culture will vanish, as all other cultures have vanished, and the cause of our destruction will be the ever-progressing materialism and egoism that will eventually culminate in a 'war of all against all'.

A small number of people, who have grasped the need for spirituality, will carry over the knowledge presented in this book, along with all other similar knowledge, to the next culture. Together they will create a new culture of spiritual and brotherly love

Introduction

Before I write about my experiences on and beyond the threshold as a child, I will describe the structure of this book and define the concepts I will use later.

As the reader now will have understood, this book is not for everybody.

It is intended as:

- a manual on crossing the threshold to the spiritual world for all who see this as a possibility;
- a book for my anthroposophical friends to discuss how to cross the threshold in a safe way;
- a book that describes the changes in the spiritual realm during the last 100 years, in reference to Rudolf Steiner's descriptions on the threshold and the different ways to cross it.

Although broad reading in theosophical and anthroposophical literature may be relevant and important as a wider foundation to the understanding of this subject, you can understand the essentials of what I want to communicate by being familiar with only a few important concepts and some background knowledge.

What needs to be explained?

The first and foremost concept we must discuss and define is the 'I'. This concept is both the easiest to understand and one of the most difficult.

The next concept we must discuss is the etheric world and etheric powers and 'streams'. One of my first spiritual experiences was when I experienced these strange, living, black and hollow snake-like etheric connections between trees. I will describe these further in Chapter One, but here I will define these streaming lines as consisting of etheric energy; a life-giving, growth-promoting energy that is the foundation of all life.

In this etheric world, we will also find the phenomenon of 'time', which I experience as threefold: the so-called time-line, the time-spiral and the time-double-stream. While elaborating on the etheric timeline, I will later discuss the possibility of time travel.

Above or around the etheric world we find the astral world. This is very different from the etheric and contains all our feelings, our emotions and the ability to travel within it. In this world, we find the first creation of the 'I', namely the soul.

Further, we will encounter the very important concepts of the soul, soul-fragments and soul-forces, into which the 'I' can travel or project itself through our directed consciousness.

In this connection, we must discuss and be acquainted with the concept of 'dividing', as this expression is used mostly in connection with the soul-forces of thinking, feeling and will. These can be divided, just as parts of the etheric or astral bodies can be divided from the whole.

It is by means of these separated parts that the 'I' can travel or 'see' through our spiritual sense organs into the spiritual world.

When these soul forces are separated and floating out in the spiritual world, we must have a chord between them and our mind, so that the fragments do not drift away. This is called the silver cord.

In the fourth chapter we will also see that the 'I' can experience consciously the 'void' *between* the separated parts, especially between the disease-promoting forces, where the divine, angelic forces or entities can emerge. I will describe this in connection with the fight against the curse of cancer.

In short, we must become acquainted with the realm of the etheric forces, into which our etheric body is interwoven, and the realm of the astral forces, in which out astral body is immersed.

We must be acquainted with the concept of 'spiritual sense organs', counterparts of which exist in the physical, etheric and astral bodies. These sense organs can be developed, focused and extended to encompass greater parts of both the soul and the body, as well as the whole universe. I imagine that this subject will be the most difficult to comprehend, and because of this I will discuss it in detail in Addendum 1.

We will also have to deal with other entities that we meet at or beyond the threshold, which can be perceived by the spiritual sense organs from different angles or perspectives. They are of several main types: the etheric elementals, the astral elementals and the karmic elementals. There are also the ahrimanic, the luciferic and the azuric elementals, which are named 'demons', 'spectres' or 'phantoms' when they are destructive to man and nature. When they are not destructive or 'demonic', they are necessary in order to fulfil our karma, our development as human beings and our freedom of will. We also have nature elementals of earth, water, air and fire, as well as elementals related to flowers and trees.

Further, we will meet the concepts of the 'Guardian of the Threshold', the 'Animals of the Threshold', the 'Abyss of the Threshold' and the ahrimanic, the luciferic, the azuric and the karmic doppelgängers or 'doubles'.

On the other side, we will also meet the good spiritual beings: our guardian angels and the rest of the angelic hierarchies. We will meet the advanced spiritual teachers and the initiated human beings.

We may meet the cosmic intelligence, called Sophia, the Christ force and lastly the high trinity of all Creation, the Father, the Mother and the Child or Holy Spirit.

Why I describe the adversaries, demons and frightening aspects first is because I met them first in my personal path through the spirit world, probably due to my karma. However, on several occasions in my life I met the good forces, but more in instances of individual need.

When I learned to divide the adversarial forces and to look behind them, I came to experience the divine and good forces and entities of the spiritual world.

Definitions

I will try now, at the beginning of this book, to explain and describe in detail what I mean by all these concepts, otherwise the reader may soon be left in darkness and confusion.

The physical body

This is not as simple as we might at first believe, in either its material or spiritual aspects. In the context of this book, we have to understand the concept of awakening the 'I' in different parts of the physical body. When we awaken our consciousness within a defined and restricted area of the physical body (as well as the other 'bodies' that we will discuss later), we will find that different parts of the body contain different portals to the spiritual world.

The etheric body

This gives life to the physical body. This etheric body is a manifold and complex structure of flowing and streaming currents of living energy, which connect us to the formative forces in the plant world as well as to the totality of these forces in the cosmos. This body can be used as a gateway into the etheric realm of reality, and it contains spiritual sense organs. These organs are developed either directly or as a template influenced from the astral body.

If the etheric body is weakened, alien spirits will be able to possess the void of the etheric. If these entities are malignant, we call them demons. These are primarily ahrimanic demons. Such demons lead to sclerotic processes in their host.

The etheric world is a world that contains the life force of the entire cosmos, the force that makes energy appear in the void and that gives life to all. This etheric world encompasses all that is alive, and it fills us with this life force. In trees, this world can be observed by the life it gives to them, and can be seen with the spiritual and clairvoyant 'eye' as dark and snake-like flowing streams of energy between trees. That is how I see it.

I will now discuss these dark and snake-like connections between trees. For me, they were difficult to understand in the beginning, but many years later I came to a deeper understanding. The black snakes are living in the etheric world, which is a world of growth forces that are used both by humans as a source of thinking and by trees as a means of communicating. Trees communicate in a time-free fashion, and later I discovered that by entering these hollow snakes with my consciousness, I was able to 'travel' back in time, together with the trees. I can also travel back in time using other etheric streams, like those found in the human body, the animals, the earth itself or in the cosmos.*

The astral body
The astral body is that part of supersensible man and animals that deals with feelings and movement. Plants do not have an astral body, except for the poisonous ones, which influence the astral body, and in some cases the etheric body, and these are of special interest here.

This body sets us in relation or connects us to the astral world, the animal world and the cosmic counterparts of these forces. The astral body forms and influences the etheric body, and also contains the first beginnings of the soul.

If the astral body is weakened, it will be possible for luciferic forces, spirits or demons to enter the astral void, and such possession will lead to dissolving diseases, infections and hysteric states of mind.

The soul
The soul, the soul-fragments and the soul-forces are important to understand fully. When the conscious I works upon the different areas of the astral, etheric or physical body, the parts that are made conscious are called the soul. Thus, the soul consists of three parts:

---

*There is more about these techniques later in this book.

- the sentient soul, developed from the astral body;
- the intellectual soul, developed from the etheric body;
- the consciousness soul, developed from the physical body.

These parts are intertwined in the material world, just as the astral, etheric and physical bodies are intertwined, and as such also imprison us in this material world. If we can free the different parts of the soul from this entwinement, we can use these fragments to step over the threshold and to explore the spiritual world. The important thing here is to stay with the conscious I within these fragments of the soul, otherwise alien influences may enter, and that is not good. Not good at all.

The 'I'

I have already explained the 'I' above, but I will repeat the definition again briefly. The 'I' is the very function in our spiritual selves that we experience, when we say I or 'myself', as our self-conscious, central core of identity. It can enter all realms of the spiritual, the etheric, the astral and even the physical. The 'I' is the divine spark or fire inside ourselves and is both dependent and independent of the body, as during sleep, when it travels outside our body.

With this 'I', we can consciously 'travel' both inside and outside the body and explore different parts of it. We can visit foreign places in the cosmos, travel in time and direct both energetic streams, geopathic earth-radiation and the soul forces called thinking, feeling and will.

The 'I' is thus of immense power and of unlimited possibilities. I realized this power as a child, when I experienced that a sore throat healed in a few minutes when I placed my consciousness, or 'I', in the throat. The 'I' can thus move and direct the pathological entities or functions in the body, through suppression, translocation and transformation (more of this in Chapter 4).

The conscious 'I' works in and through the physical, etheric and astral bodies, creating what we may call the 'soul', a soul that is conscious through our conscious thinking in the etheric body, our half-conscious feeling in the astral body, and our almost unconscious will in the physical body. When these three faculties are intertwined, time is created and can be experienced as a fourth function of space.

As I experience this, the soul thus contains four main functions, and within each of them, there are multiple subfunctions. These four functions are *thinking, feeling, will* and *time*. Through them and their subfunctions, we may perceive the spiritual world, create portals into the

spiritual world, travel into this world or become active with our consciousness—our I-function—in this world, through the awakened spiritual sense organs. To be able to operate these parts of the soul, we have to
separate a function from the 'whole', from the rest of the body.

Spirit is that part of the 'I'-consciousness that man has received from
the great cosmic spirit-sea, also called God.

The three time-qualities and time travelling

In my experience, time is closely linked to the etheric world and the
etheric communication and connection between individuals, especially
between trees. I will now try to describe and define time as I see and
experience it beyond the threshold. I must emphasize that this is not a
construct of theory or philosophy, but the direct experience that started
when I was around 40 years old. The observations were made while
experimenting with the dark rivers of etheric energy streaming between
trees.

At first, I just observed these streams, how they, as living beings, bound
together all the trees, groups of trees, animals, and even the humans in a
vast and cosmic network of living energy. Then, when I 'entered' these
streams, it was a strange and foreign world. I actually entered the streams
in that I physically stepped into them and stood in the middle of the
streaming dark energy. Then I found out that they were hollow, and that
I could go into the middle of the streams with my liberated consciousness
or 'I'.

There I both saw and experienced that inside, the streams were flowing
in two directions, one to the right and one to the left. If I floated with the
streaming etheric force to the left, I went further and further into the past.
When I floated to the right, I went into the future. I never dared to go far
into the future, but I often drifted far into the past. One strange thing was
that, if I entered the stream from the other side, 'left' still brought me to
the past, even if 'left' was now 'right'.

What I experienced there in the past was the history of the trees or the
plants, and I drifted back as far as to the Silurian Period.

> I saw the old clouds soaring across the sky,
> the Sun sending her light down to the earth,
> and the stars talking their ancient and silent language.
> I saw it from above, 80 million years ago.
> However, I woke from this special feeling,
> and these old times disappeared.

The old times when the earth conceived
the sunlight with innocence.
When the earth was still an altar,
not a grave.
When humanity itself was only
a star glimmering thought.

It was often difficult to come back to the present after such emotional experiences.

In this way, I experienced the double stream of time. If I followed the stream back in time, there were two different ways to travel:

- One that took me straight back endlessly, without a deeper understanding of cause and effect in what happened. This was a linear time-line.

- One that transported me back in such a way that I could understand what happened and why. This type of travel was in spirals, so I could understand how the 'arms' of the spiral influenced the next 'arm', and that each 'round' was a higher repetition of the last.

Soul Fragments

The separation of soul-fragments needs a deep and thorough explanation. The general technique of passing the threshold is through achieving this division. We are held as prisoners in the material world because our body and soul are held together by strong forces, almost like atoms in a molecule. These bonds bind us to the illusion that the physical/material world is the only true reality, governed by space and time.

It seems to me that anything can be divided, and therefore this opens innumerable portals and ways that lead over the threshold and into the spiritual world. However, I must state and emphasize clearly that, to be able to divide the deeply connected thinking, feeling and will, we have to know what these really are. We must train ourselves to know what our thinking, our feeling and our will really are.

Also, it is very important to understand what Lucifer and Ahriman[*] truly represent. However—and here comes a contradictory statement— to really know these three soul abilities or the adversaries defined as Lucifer and Ahriman, we have to divide them, at least a little, so as to understand how they act as a singularity. This training must thus go in parallel; we must divide a little in order to see what each part or entity

---

[*] These two adversarial beings will be explained later in this Introduction.

really is and get to know the individual powers better—then we divide further, then understand deeper, and so on. This took me many years.

But how do we divide, how do we separate? Such a separation occurred automatically for me from my earliest memory, but I did not become conscious of it before I was five or six years old. In the beginning, I tried to stop this separation, as it frightened me to 'lose reality'. Then I started to enjoy the separation, as it was a means of experiencing something different and exciting, although at that time I did not believe in any *objective* spiritual world; I thought it was all going on only inside my brain, as a *subjective* experience.

At the age of 21, I realized that this spiritual world was objective, and started to take a deeper interest in the dividing, to analyse the method and discover how this division came about.

At the age of 33, I decided to halt the automatic ability to divide, which I initiated by inserting a small needle in my ear, which resulted in a huge explosion inside my head. I had to analyse the method and develop a conscious way to separate the 'soul-fragments'. Afterwards, I had to analyse carefully what I had done, or what my soul had done by itself, before my decision to 'take over' the procedure of separation.

Then I realized that the important part of the procedure of division was to let the part that was to be separated, 'die'. I had to 'pretend' that one part of me had died, and to feel death invading this part.

- If a part of the thinking is left to die, I feel that the thinking gets darker, and this darkness will invade my thinking from the sides.
- If I let a part of my feeling die, I feel that a sort of coldness invades my chest area from the front.
- If I let a part of my will die, I feel that a kind of death invades my body from below.
- If I let part of my physical body die, I feel like the nerve supply fails in this area; as if it 'sleeps' away.
- If I let a part of my etheric body 'sleep' (that is the most difficult), I have to 'drain' the life force out of the area or organ in question, much like the death of the will, although the draining of the etheric force feels more 'lethal' than the death of the will.
- When I let a part of my astral body die, I feel I become immobile, as if all movement has left me.
- When I let a part of the time-line die (whether it is the past, the future, the straight-lined time or the spiralled time) I feel as if I am alone, having lost all friends or connections.

When the part is in a state of partial death or sleep, the opening is made for the conscious 'I' to enter. The 'I' is then already in connection with the awakened sense organ, whether sight, hearing or feeling. Then I can observe a part of the spiritual world through the combined action of the conscious 'I', the void or death-state of the fragment, and the awakened spiritual sense organ, of which there are twelve.

★

When I was 62 years old, I discovered an even more interesting and promising way of division relating to finding the 'Middle Point'.

I found that everything that exists in the material world is dependent on and has to consist of the forces of Lucifer and Ahriman, including man himself. All life forms, all man-made machines, all electronic devices and mobile phones, consist of these two forces. Between these two forces, we can find the Christ force or consciousness. In dividing these forces of Lucifer and Ahriman, we can create a space for the Christ, and this can have far-reaching consequences regarding disease, mental health and even the pathological effects of electromagnetic radiation from mobile phones, 4 and 5G masts, or other electronic/electro-magnetic installations.

If I apply this kind of dividing to myself by creating a greater distance between my own luciferic and ahrimanic internal entities or 'demons', I am able to open my heart to Christ and the angelic forces that accompany this force. This has brought a new dimension to my life, that earlier was occupied mostly by the understanding of and fight against demonic entities. Nowadays I can open to the good forces also.

In connection with the understanding of 'dividing something', I will remind the reader that the passing of the threshold to the spiritual world in life is very much like the transition after death. I will thus refer to how Rudolf Steiner described this transition—how everything we are will then be divided:

> Then, when the etheric body has been abandoned, another very remarkable feeling arises. It is really difficult to describe this feeling in words drawn from the physical world. It is a feeling of expansion into wide cosmic space but as though one were not actually within every place. The experience can only be described approximately. The individual feels as though with one part of his being he were in Munich, with another part of his being in Mainz, with a third in Basel, and with another far outside the Earth sphere, perhaps in the Moon. He feels as though he were dismembered, as though he were not

connected with the spaces in between. That is the peculiar way of experiencing oneself as an astral being, spread out in space, transferred to different centres, but not filling the regions between them.[*]

The Silver Cord
The 'silver cord' is of special importance when any soul-fragment or other faculty including the 'I' is separated from the body and then travels afar. This soul-fragment can be 'lost' out there in the spiritual world and not be taken back into the totality of the soul. In shamanistic cultures, and especially the Sami culture, this losing of different soul-fragments is considered one of the main reasons for disease, especially diseases of the mind. The shaman has then to enter the spiritual world to find the lost soul-fragment of his patient, and take this fragment back ('soul retrieval'). Such a journey can be dangerous, and the shaman has to take precautions in order to travel safely.

Spiritual Sense Organs
The spiritual sense organs are also of special importance and interest in this book, and I was not aware of their existence until I reached the age of 21. I thought that I saw the spiritual with my physical sense organs, and could not understand why everybody didn't see what I saw. I hear quite often that clairvoyants claim that they can see the spiritual beings through their 'real eyes' or 'real ears'. This is not true, although it may sometimes feel that way.

Gradually, I understood that the physical sense organs also have their spiritual equivalents that are activated when we separate the area of the sense organ. For example, if I separate the feeling from the area around the eye, I can 'see' something astral, but if I separate the thinking from the area around the eye, I can see something etheric, as the astral is related to the feeling whereas thinking is related to the etheric. According to Rudolf Steiner, there are twelve sense organs, situated all over the body, so that we may separate both thinking, feeling or will from any part of the body and obtain a spiritual view of the spiritual world or some part of it. It is important, though, that we do this consciously, with our 'I' present, otherwise we can open to the adversarial forces.

With the physical body, the etheric body, the astral body, the different time-functions and the described soul-properties, we have the instruments for our passing of the threshold. As these instruments are manifold,

---

[*] *Theosophy of the Rosicrucian,* lecture 7, given on 31 May 1907 (GA 99).

we therefore have innumerable ways of passing this threshold. We also have the possibility to divide the adversaries and thus create another portal into the spiritual world, especially the angelic or archangelic worlds.

The concept of the adversaries is probably the most alien to the reader but it is one of the most important areas of knowledge, especially when we travel to the other side of the threshold and actually face an evil entity or a demon.

If we stay put on the material side of the threshold, we are safe, although we are constantly under the influence of the adversarial forces, especially the ahrimanic. Once we cross the threshold, we are no longer safe, and we need to guard ourselves with the help of knowledge, love, faith and hope.

In the spiritual world, on the other side of the threshold, there are many entities, and these entities are of different types, just as in the physical world. Here in the physical world, we may meet innumerable types of beings; some are beneficial to us, some are indifferent and some are dangerous. In the spiritual world it is just as in the physical world, and the beings or entities that are dangerous to us we call 'adversaries'.

There are many different types of adversaries, but to make it easier to define them we may split them into three groups:

- the ahrimanic beings,
- the luciferic beings,
- the azuric beings.

I wrote earlier that if we are not conscious within our separated parts, with our awakened I, then alien and malignant forces may enter. A meeting with these powers seems to be inevitable when working with crossing the threshold and going into the spiritual world.

In the spiritual world there are:

- demons, which are ahrimanic adversarial entities in the etheric realm,
- spectres, which are luciferic adversarial entities in the astral realm,
- phantoms, which are azuric adversarial entities in the physical realm, and attack the physical body as well as the 'I'.

Today, the ahrimanic beings are the most dangerous, just as in the far past it was the luciferic beings and in the future it will be the azuras.

When using drugs, especially hallucinogenic drugs, we open up to the following entities:

- the ahrimanic powers, which want us to be more materialistic and deny the spiritual world;
- the luciferic powers, which want us to lose ourselves in our own subjective experiences of the spiritual world; and
- the azuric powers, which want us to lose our I, or make the 'I' egoistic and unusable in the spiritual world.

Rudolf Steiner describes the following entities or phenomena in his 19 Class lectures:[*]

- the guardian of the threshold,
- animals of the threshold,
- the abyss of the threshold,
- ahrimanic doppelgängers,
- luciferic doppelgängers,
- azuric doppelgängers,
- karmic doppelgängers.

They are all creatures or projections from our own soul—projections that warn, instruct and prepare us to be mature enough to take the step over the threshold.

I myself have not experienced these phenomena in the same way as described by Steiner, and I suspect they appear a little different now than in 1924. Also, it might be different when a child experiences and gets acquainted with these entities than when one experiences them for the first time as an adult. In addition, it appears that everyone experiences these phenomena slightly differently, according to the spiritual law set forth by Heraclites: that everything is in a constant state of flux.

Bearing this in mind, below I describe how I have experienced these beings.

The *guardian of the threshold* is an entity that stands before the abyss of the threshold in order to remind us of the dangers involved and to instruct us as to what to do and what not do when passing the threshold; or even that we must wait if we are not mature enough. I do not remember having met this entity consciously, as I crossed the threshold before I lived a conscious life.

The *animals of the threshold* are projections of our own undeveloped thinking, feeling and will. They are there to remind us that when we separate the soul-faculties, we will see them as they are, full of faults,

---

[*]Published as *The First Class Lessons and Mantras: The Michael School Meditative Path in Nineteen Steps*, held in Dornach between 15 February and 2 August 1924 (GA 270).

mistakes, lies and weaknesses. If we don't accept or recognize these faults before we pass the threshold, the adversaries will use them in their own play for power, and we will be lost to their forces.

I have met these animals consciously, as described in Chapter 2 relating to thinking, and Chapter 3 relating to the Irish experience at Longford. I have had encounters with them in thinking, feeling and will.

The *abyss of the threshold* is described by Rudolf Steiner as a deep abyss over which we need to grow wings to pass. In my experience, this is not as deep and difficult to pass as described by him, but that is probably due to my early crossing.

Rudolf Steiner describes the ahrimanic, luciferic, azuric and karmic doppelgängers as the shadow pictures respectively of our etheric body, astral body, 'I'-organization and karma. In my experience, this is to accept your diseases (stemming from the etheric body), your mental disturbances (coming from the astral body), your faults (originating in the 'I') and also the place, family and birth circumstances, which are the result of karma. To accept all of this is to accept who you really are.

The good, helping and beneficial beings that I have met throughout life have been considerably fewer and more hidden than the malevolent beings that I have had to resist or even fight. This is probably due to my karma, and I was not able to see or meet the light-filled, good and helping part of the spiritual world until the more sinister parts of this karma were resolved. As described in my book *The Forgotten Mysteries of Atlantis*, the last part of my sinister karma was resolved in meeting 'L' in 2011 and 'H' in the late autumn of 2014, from which time I was able to work my way into the benevolent part of the spiritual world. The question posed by my friend 'M' was very important: 'Why don't you open up more to the angels?', which I then did.

Help for going forward and for bearing the sufferings of the material world or karma can be obtained from such entities as:

- the natural elemental beings of:
  - *Water,*
  - Air,
  - *Earth,*
  - *Fire*;
- the Initiates, such as:
  - *Christian Rosenkreutz,*
  - *Rudolf Steiner,*
  - *Master Jesus*;

- the teachers of wisdom, such as:
  - The old Moon beings,
  - *Sophia*;
- the angels, such as:
  - *The guardian angels*,
  - The common angels,
  - The Archangels;
- the Christ,
- Mary,
- God,

(The entities marked in italics refer to those whom I have met and have been helped by.)

1. Childhood (6–12)

In this first part, I will try to stay true to the consciousness of a child, and describe my way and experiences as they appeared to me at that age. I will thus describe that 'something left my soul' and other such somewhat diffuse phrases.

With the background and descriptions in the foregoing introduction, I hope that the reader will be able to understand what I attempt to describe, to make some sense of it and to understand my development.

★

One of the first things I can remember in my life is watching parts of my inner being, my soul, leaving me, and thereby feeling that reality had also left me and that I was all alone.

It was not I who floated out of the body (this happened many years later), but part of my soul. As the Sami people describe it, soul-fragments can disappear. If they then get lost, the result is disease or madness, or different inabilities. However, during this process, if they are continually kept under control, they may become powerful tools in spiritual development. There is always a thin silver cord between the soul-fragments or abilities and yourself. This cord does not break easily.

Later in life, I learned from Sami shamans that most people with psychic disturbances have lost such soul-parts, and that they cannot find them again. Then, as described earlier, the shaman must travel into the spiritual world to find them and bring them back to the disturbed person. Many physical diseases are also considered to have this cause by the Sami shaman.

In my case, these parts always came back; I never lost control over them. The silver cord was always strong.

In the beginning, I did not want these parts to leave me, and found that applying a certain rhythm helped to keep them inside and contained.

My first remembrance of this 'losing of soul-parts' was at a family party. I was around five-years-old. After drumming my hands on the table for a while, my father asked me why I was doing this. I still remember my answer clearly: '*So that I will not lose reality.*' My father looked at me and told me to stop talking such nonsense. I never said anything like that again.

The next time I mentioned this leaving-of-soul-faculties was when I was enlisted to be a 'bomb shelter guard' in Northern Norway, which was part of civil defence training in case of war. I was then 30-years-old and already working as a veterinarian. I told the female commander-in-chief that in situations when I was in danger, I had the tendency to excarnate parts of my soul, especially relating to my will to act, and then I was of no use to anyone. She looked at me for almost five minutes and then asked me if I had told anyone about this before. I said that I had not. She thought for some more minutes and then told me to go home.

Let us now return to myself as the little boy, who so easily saw his soul-faculties travel by themselves into the wide expanses of the world.

At a very early age, I learned by trial and error how I could make the different soul-properties leave, and how I could hinder this happening, and this has been the key for my spiritual investigation later in life. All investigations, all my diagnostic work and all my therapeutic work, have been performed in or from the spiritual world. That is why such results cannot be reproduced in a laboratory or experimental setting.

The first thing I learned about this excarnation of parts of my soul was that if I was in some kind of imbalance, it became easier. Having an infection, especially the flu, I could more easily excarnate different parts. Also, after small shocks or unexpected happenings, it was very easy to loosen and excarnate.

The second thing I learned was that the departing part had to be changed somewhat in order to be able to free itself from the rest of the body and soul. At that time, I did this by letting these parts 'go to sleep'— to enter slightly into a death-like state.[*] I could still follow and stay in contact with them, which was a faculty I developed further in my years as a veterinarian. This became a central part of my diagnostic protocol and later also part of my therapeutic system.

As I got more and more practice in splitting off separate parts of my soul or etheric body (life forces), the different parts that I could split off increased in number, from one in the beginning to two, three, four or more.

Relatively early, I could feel four different, distinct parts of the soul that were able to leave me, to excarnate. I could separate these parts either one at a time, or two, three or four together. This fourfoldness was very accurate and obvious for me. There was never a doubt in my mind that I had four functions that could leave me and then come back, often with some kind of insight or information from the 'other world'.

---

[*] As Henrik Ibsen wrote: 'To kill oneself is to find oneself.'

Usually, my feeling parted first, then after five minutes my thinking, then again after five minutes my will, and lastly time itself. I felt and experienced these four separated functions of the soul very differently; they felt and acted quite differently, both inside and outside me.

- One of the soul-parts, usually the first one to separate, had to do with experiencing the distance to my surroundings, whether they were close or far away. When this first part was still anchored in my soul and not yet separated, I could easily estimate how far away any object was. If this part left me, I was no longer able to fathom the distance of people or things. This was actually quite a funny phase in the passing of the threshold. I could then imagine that what I looked upon was far away, and then I could experience that it was immensely big—as if a fly on the table was 10 km away and therefore must be enormously huge and dangerous. This gave me a sense of excitement. If I looked upon a friend and imagined that he was very close, then he had to be very small.

The joys of a child! The farther this soul-part excarnated from me, the more difficult it became to judge distances, and the whole of reality seemed to fade away. As this happened, my thinking and feeling followed or seemed to follow the fading away, so that my intellectual thinking and reasoning became 'un-intelligent'. It became more and more difficult to think logically, although to think in pictures and in parables became increasingly easy.

- The next function that tended to leave me was the ability to act and move. At this level or stage, I had to stop walking, working or doing anything physical. This part had to do with the strength or weakness of my body. I felt either immensely strong or immensely weak.
- The third soul-function that tended to leave me had to do with my heart—if I felt content or happy. When this part left, I felt alone in the universe. When it came back, I felt blessed with feeling at one with all, a sort of cosmic, altruistic feeling. When I concentrated on the silver chord that connected this to the rest of me, I did not feel so alone. After I learned to operate through this part within the cosmos, I did not feel alone at all, but that was at a later time in my life.

My first poem, written at the age of six, was about this feeling of one-ness:

If everybody is happy
then 'all' is happy.
When the animals in the forest
drink from the happy water,
the water is happy that it may
merge with the happy animals.
And then the sand on which
the animals are standing
is also happy.

- The last soul-part had to do with time, the *experience* of time; if it flowed fast, slow, or ceased to exist at all. To see time itself leaving me, when I was little, was the most difficult thing to understand, and at times it could be quite frightening. Later in my life, this phase of the passing of the threshold became the most 'interesting', as I could then move freely into the past, which I experienced as 'time-travelling'. If this part excarnated far enough out into the cosmic expanses, time ceased to exist completely, at least for me. Then I floated, not in space, but in time itself. Later in life, I learned how this part could separate as a single ability. By travelling in time, I am not referring to imaginations of past times; it actually felt like I *was* there. I could sit with open eyes and actually see old knights pass by. At first I got scared, but after some time I learned that my body was not actually present within the experience—it was only my spiritual and immortal soul, or a fragment of it—and that nobody could hurt me in this travelling state. Then I could quietly sit down and watch the old dinosaurs pass by. Sometimes I was filled with a fear of not coming back, that I would be stuck in those far-off times, but I found a method to get back, which was actually like that used by Sami shamans to return to the body if they were lost in their search for lost 'soul-fragments'.

This was what I knew in my childhood.

The next stage of my learning was how to follow the soul-parts into the cosmos. I could then choose if I wanted to stay behind in the body, or go with the separated parts into the cosmos.

It is very important in all spiritual work to be able to choose where to be with your consciousness. Self-consciousness—the feeling and knowledge of being yourself, of being in *thine own* 'I'—is extremely important. The silver cord that connects you with all your soul-fragments is actually the 'I' itself.

Throughout Rudolf Steiner's writings, the 'I' has a central place, and he describes how it is a gift from the Gods and the function that keeps the human being together. It is through the 'I' that we eventually will be able to transform our soul and even our body to become a *spiritual human being*, to reach what the Indians call 'Atma', or 'spirit man' in anthroposophy.

If the 'I'-organization—which inhabits the warmth of the blood, the centre of the brain (behind the eyes) and the chambers of the heart—is weakened, it is dangerous to separate the soul-fragments, cross the threshold and enter into the spiritual world. Without the strength and consciousness of the 'I', the result of such a crossing can be like what Dirk Kruse described in his experience of crossing.[*] If the 'I' is strong and conscious enough, nothing can happen to you.

There are many stories about people who crossed the threshold—or rather separated the soul-fragments—who could not bear the experiences that they were forced to endure. In the 'Sami' culture of Northern Scandinavia, such an aetiology is considered the most common in diseases, especially in psychiatric conditions. The shaman's job is then to go into the spiritual world to find and bring back these fragments. In diseases that are more common, the situation is the opposite, but still related to a weak 'I'. In many ordinary diseases, the spiritual aspect of the human being is invaded by foreign soul-fragments, often called and experienced as 'demons'[†] or disease entities. These entities can be seen by the clairvoyant and treated or driven out, but if the 'I' is strong enough, such alien forces will not be allowed to enter in the first place.

So how does one know that the 'I' is strong enough to enter the spiritual world? One actually doesn't know until one has tried. There are some indications, however:

- The ability to continue to work, although the work is boring, reflects the strength of the 'I'.
- The ability to stay awake, although sleep is pressing, reflects the same.
- The ability to resist temptation also reflects the strength of the 'I'. That is why the three temptations of Christ in the desert are of utmost importance in the Gospels.

If one feels the slightest tendency to lose control over the soul-fragments while passing the threshold, one should retract and wait for a later pos-

---

[*] In 'Between Suicide and Madness' (not really an uplifting title!), a lecture Kruse held in Schafwinkel, Germany, in 1995.

[†] See my book *Demons and Healing*, Temple Lodge, 2018.

sibility. I have myself lost this control a few times, and then I had to struggle for about half an hour—which seemed to be a long time in that situation, although in the physical world this is not really much time—to come back and regain control.

★

I will now describe what happened inside my 'brain', blood or heart-chambers when one or more soul-fragments left (and this is the same for me now). The only difference is that, as a child, it happened involuntarily, whereas now I can make it happen by will (but more on this technique later in Chapter 4).

In my 'I'-organization, I experience many functions. These are ordered in compartments: for example, thinking, feeling, will and time. These compartments cooperate with each other and intermingle, although in essence they are independent. Sometimes, therefore, I feel like a multi-person being, as if I were several persons within myself, and that these persons could change from one to another within seconds. When one of these faculties separates, it divides from the rest and also from 'me'. When it divides from me, it leaves the others and creates freedom for itself, and *also for the place in the brain, heart or blood where it was originally resting.*

I call this its 'anchor place' within the body. Here, a residue remains, a kind of nucleus which seems to be the part of this faculty that has become conscious through the work of the 'I'. If several or all of these functions are separated at the same time, they stay by themselves; they do not mix unless I mix them through control of the 'I' from the nucleus, the anchor-place inside my brain.

This nucleus was the first anchoring place I discovered. I could not manage such control for long periods when I was a child. Later, I was able to mix these functions, but not before I reached the age of 30.

As a child, when one 'fragment' separated, I could choose to stay inside my own body—inside what was left—or I could go inside and through this nucleus. That was my connection to the excarnated part, in order to see and experience through the excarnated faculty. I could go into this particular quality of soul and investigate it closer in its cosmic life.

I literally 'see' these functions imaginatively, within my spiritual eye. I 'see' the function leave the other functions, and at the same time it separates within itself, leaving a smaller part of itself free within my head, heart or blood. The remaining part or parts become more and more condensed as the main parts dissolve into the cosmos.

The more the departed faculty fills the whole cosmos, the more the remaining nucleus—whether in my brain, heart and blood (in the limbs)—feels like conscious thinking, conscious feeling, or conscious will respectively. These nuclei remain as very condensed points deep in either my brain, heart or limbs. Through them, I can activate all my spiritual sense organs, which can then use the dissolved, cosmic parts of the faculty to think, feel, act, observe, or just be conscious.

From quite early on, it became apparent that the onset of separation had to do with the horizontal direction. If I entered into the surroundings with my mind, my intention or my sight, and faded into the distance—as we sometimes do when we daydream or fade away during a boring lecture (for me the first time being a boring family gathering)—then I could watch the first part departing, with the others following soon afterwards.

One important aspect of this dividing is that it has a double function, a double dividing that has a cross form. When, for example, the first part goes out into the periphery (which is mainly to the left and the right) and splits from the remaining parts, it also divides from the nucleus—a sort of mirror image within myself. The remaining condensed or changed nucleus seems to radiate or stream from the front to the back. These two divisions occur in opposite directions, thus forming a cross. I can observe this streaming, energetic or spiritual cross in persons that are able to enter the spiritual world.

In puberty, I also became more aware of the temptations of this spiritual path, which can be many. I will discuss them in more detail later.

★

Being a child, I really did not understand all this. I just played with it and kept quiet about it, even to my friends. I have decided to talk about my childhood experiences here for the first time.

So, how did I induce this separation, and how did I choose to be in one, two, or three of the 'I'-conscious nuclei described? How did I make the faculties come back, and how did I prevent them from going out? As a child, I did not do this at all, it just happened and I followed the best I could. Only later was I able to do this consciously, with purpose.

At first, I only played with this dividing and the experience of going into the spiritual world. But just as a baby learns to walk, so I learnt to navigate in this other realm and to master a certain dominion over both separation and its hindrance.

I also learned about the importance of nature. I was always very fond of nature—the trees, the flowers and the birds and animals—and I often went out alone into the woods at a very early age, and my father encouraged me to do so. At the age of 12, I went on my own into the woods to spend the night there, and I slept many a night with the sky over my head, accompanied by the sounds of the owls and animals around me.

When I grew older, and especially after I had children of my own, I realized that others were not as much in love with nature as I was. I spent a lot of time trying to understand why, even as late as 1979, in the veterinary school of Oslo, where many of my classmates were pre-occupied with wilderness sports and hunting. A hunter shows a seeming love for nature, but that sort of love was not what I felt at all. I tried to understand why other people's relationship to nature was mostly different to mine. Of course, some people have as close and intimate a relationship to nature as I do, but it is somewhat rare.

Today, I think that I can understand my love and close relationship to nature by learning about the goddess Natura. Rudolf Steiner talks much about the help that the initiates of olden times, especially before the twelfth century, received from the goddess.[*] This goddess lives in the etheric realm of nature, and taught the old initiates about the elements, the forces and life in the great and abundant natural world.

I imagine that I was close to the goddess Natura when I grew up, as I felt the life in all animals and flowers and insects. I strongly felt the urge to protect them from hunters, from modern society and from pain. All my life up to the present, I have felt this urge to protect.

I lived in the presence of the etheric world, which I actually saw in the 'parting' of my soul. I am sure that I received a lot of help and instruction from nature, from the goddess Natura.

So, as a child, what did I learn from this work concerning the method of entering the spiritual world, which I am endeavouring to write down here? I learned about the help I could get from:

- Nature,
- trees,
- the directions of space,
- letting parts of myself die,
- and the controlling function of the 'I'.

*

The next riddle or mystery I met in my childhood was the ability to *see through flesh*, in particular the hands of other people, but also later, as a

---

[*] See his lecture series *True and False Paths in Spiritual Investigation* held in 1924 (GA 243).

veterinarian, to be able to see through the huge body of a horse and find areas of trauma or scars. I was unable to comprehend how this ability came about, until I consciously divided the will from the rest of my soul abilities.

I will now try to describe what I did and how such sight shows itself within my brain or behind my physical eyes. When I want to look at what is inside a fist, a horse's body or other physical body parts, I have two possible ways:

The first way is to separate my will from the other two soul-faculties. Then I direct my I-consciousness through the separated will inside my own fist, hand or the body-part through which I want to look. Using my own hand or body-part, I then look outside to the fist or the body-part of the other person, after which an image of what is behind the skin appears. I see it in close proximity to, and slightly behind, my physical eyes. *The other way* is to let the body part in question 'die' without going through the will, and then to let the spiritual sense organ look directly into the patient's body part. I have been able to perfect this last process so that I let my whole body die somewhat, and then 'scan' the whole body of the patient. If I then see something interesting, I can repeat the procedure relating to the more specific body part, and thus take a closer look at it.

Later, I learned through experience that I could always go through a part of my own body to penetrate into the equivalent area of another being, be it an animal or a human or, at times, even a tree or stone. One morning, on 1 January, at the top of the Atlas Mountains, I was able to gaze straight through the whole Earth itself using this technique.

What did these faculties do to me as a child and what benefits did I receive from all of this, apart from the interesting play, learning and some knowledge? The practical abilities I remember from my childhood were that I could:

- see through my father's hands, and thus know in which hand my father held the black pawn when playing chess;
- foresee the weather the next day;
- know when somebody close to me had died.

These abilities baffled my father quite a lot, especially when we played chess. It also puzzled him that on many occasions I was able to tell him what he would have to do on the next day at work, as I knew if it would rain or snow. My mother, however, was not baffled by any of this. She just seemed to accept it, perhaps because she was absorbed in Spiritualism. In a certain way, it did still amaze me that she did not ask me anything about what I did or said.

One morning, for example, when I was around seven years old, the telephone rang. I knew then that someone close to me was dead, and as my father was at our cabin in the countryside, I feared that it might be him. When my mother came up to my bedroom in tears, telling me that my grandfather had died, I exclaimed, 'Oh, that's good' (meaning that it was good that it was not my father). She never asked me why I was so happy that her father was dead, and today I am a little sad that I did not tell her.

In my relationship with both trees and the moon, I made a specific observation from the other side of the threshold. For me, the trees were persons, live creatures that stood in connection with each other and with me, and were of a high spiritual rank. In a poem some years later, I tried to describe how, as a seven-year-old, I experienced the garden outside our house. Interestingly, this poem features the intermingling between the sun, the moon and the trees, the day and the night, which one might experience in the early stage of a spiritual path. (I present it below in Norwegian, then in English translation.)

Engelen

Dørene er stengt
i den ene er det et vindu
og håndtaket er lavt nok
til å få tak
for den som ikke er stor.

Døra er åpen
og inn strømmer den nye vårlufta.
Ikke langt unna står kirsebærtreet
fylt av duft og blomster
som den hvite fullmånen.

Jeg er nyvasket
og det er lørdag.

Innved kirsebærstammen
står det en skikkelse
i månelyset.

Og selv om det er dag
og alle de andre sover middag
lyser skikkelsen i mørket.

The Angel

The doors are closed.
In one of the doors there is a little window,
and the handle is low enough
to be reached
for the one that is small.

The door is open
and the new spring-air flows in.

Not far away is the cherry-tree
filled with its smell and white flowers
as the full, white moon.

I am new washed
and it is Saturday.

Close to the cherry-tree trunk
a being is standing
in the moonlight.

And even if it is day,
and all the others are sleeping their afternoon nap,
the entity is glowing in the dark.

As I mentioned, I loved nature and animals. I rescued insects from
drowning, walked in the forest, slept outside unsupervised, and wrote
many poems about trees and animals. I was often alone.

2. Youth (12–21)

The time spent between 12 and 21 was a time when the temptations of this path started to reveal themselves. The temptation, at least for me, was the use of the separate soul powers on their own for purposes of self-aggrandizement or with the intent of obtaining egoistic goals. If one uses the separated thinking, feeling, will and time-line for egoistic purposes, the adversaries will find their path into your soul and lead you astray.

As you watch your soul-properties leave, you have the choice to see them objectively, or to remain in subjective relation to them when they are intermingled within yourself. When they are within yourself, you cannot see them objectively, but once they depart you have the unique opportunity to see them as they really are. This is called '*meeting the animals of the threshold*'.

Rudolf Steiner talked often about these three 'animals',* which he described as distorted and mutilated images of our own thinking (the red animal), feelings (the yellow animal) and will (the blue animal).

Until I was around 16, I thought that my thinking was very good and highly intelligent, and that my feelings also were as they ought to be, although quite early on I started to have doubts about this. I felt that my feelings were not really mine. Concerning my will, I was very satisfied. I did not consider the time-line to be mine at all, although it could be parted from my soul. At that time, I did not reflect upon this contradiction. Still today, I do not really understand how time can be both personal and objective, and how I can make it stop or flow in different directions by transposing it outside of myself. This is still a great enigma for me.

When seeing these soul-parts leaving, it is still possible to admire them, just as I admired them while they were inside of me. This creates an opening to the adversaries, so that they can get a hold of you, and lead you astray within the spiritual world. This is what Henrik Ibsen described as 'making a cut in the eye', so that Peer Gynt did not see the ugliness of the mountain king's daughter, but instead saw her as beautiful. If you see your own parts as they are, you might describe them as ugly, as three

---

*Especially in his teachings within the School of Spiritual Science given in the early months of 1924 (see GA 270. Also, *The First Class Lessons and Mantras: The Michael School Meditative Path in Nineteen Steps*, SteinerBooks USA).

terrible animals. You would see that your thinking is idiotic, that your feelings are greedy and that your will is egoistic.

According to Rudolf Steiner, if you don't see or understand the above, it will inevitably lead to:

- doubt and lying in your thinking (the red animal);
- hate, mocking and self-deceit in your feeling (the yellow animal);
- fear in your will (the blue animal).

They might be terrible to see as they really are, and we may prefer to keep the mote or 'log in our own eye' in order still to see them as beautiful. But if you develop:

- courage in your thinking to see the truth;
- love in your feeling for the spirit;
- hope in your will for the future;

then it is possible for you to see these three animals as they really are, and in so doing, you may free yourself from the grip of these adversaries.

Another effect of becoming free from the adversaries is that it will protect you later when you meet the elemental world, especially the demonic world, as I did after my 21st birthday.

In puberty, it is very easy to fall prey to such temptations so as not to see the faults and ugliness in yourself, and to use the soul-properties to gain power over others. In both thinking and feeling, this is obvious.

It is common to use *thinking* mendaciously for self-interest, which today is seen especially within the banking industry, and also increasingly in politics, where lying is used to obtain power.

One may use the power within *feeling* to twist and bend other people's feelings for one's own ends—to bind and use others—often in trying to manipulate the opposite sex to one's own advantage.

Will can be misused to obtain benefits in the material world. Using the will for egoistic purposes is considerably more difficult than using thinking or feeling, as one needs much more insight into the working of the will than usually is the case with 'ordinary' people. Later, in my thirties, I tried once to use my will to win a game of tennis, and the effect was so great that my opponent immediately told me that if I tried this again he would stop playing with me.

The use of *time* as a tool for self-aggrandizement is very seldom seen. This borders on black magic, and I have had the opportunity to watch it only a few times. To use it takes a lot of insight and knowledge. Misuse of these powers is mostly found in healing, where the time-line is distorted.

The simplest example is in homeopathy, where the etheric structure, the growth force, is reversed and old symptoms reappear. In making homeopathic remedies, it is possible to intervene in the time-line and to use the energy available for selfish purposes.

I have myself seen this procedure being applied twice, and the most impressive instance occurred when I visited a world-famous doctor living in New York. He could cure all types of cancer in a matter of days, and he had one hundred per cent success with groups of mice. It was incredible! His technique was to interrupt the time-line and to implant selfish wishes within this interruption. This opened a portal for Lucifer in particular, and vast amounts of energy were pulled out for the use of the luciferic adversaries. Of course, the luciferic entities signed this deal (as Mephistopheles did with Faust) by letting all cancers be healed by this technique, for it is very easy for the luciferic pathological entities to change their positions within the body. If this way of treating became standard practice, Lucifer would win a great victory.

The time soul-property can also be used to time travel in order to learn, without the intention to gain money and power, and that is the correct way. All four soul forces may be used for good, for the benefit of others, as well as being misused. This I learned in puberty, especially from the following incident.

At age 16, I had an interesting experience, which at that time seemed to be insignificant, although painful, but still it made a very deep impression in my soul, which even today I can easily re-experience. During this period of my life, I had a firm belief in my intelligence (I had not yet seen the red thinking-animal in its true form). I felt invincible and believed greatly in my intellectual abilities. The future felt great. I was doing very well at school, and set myself high goals for the future. My self-esteem was both very high and over-estimated.

One night I was at a party with some of my friends. I had been telling a girl about my life, how well it was going and how I had planned my future, no doubt giving a very inflated impression of who I was. I was telling her about the stars, literature, mathematics and nature, feeling my ego and intellect to be invincible. She then asked in admiration, 'Is there nothing that you don't know or can't do?' I thought for a moment and answered, 'I cannot do stenography ... yet.' One of my friends who was listening to the conversation then exclaimed, 'Are! ...', and in one second I *saw* what I was doing, where I was going and where I came from, and felt enormous shame. I saw the red animal in its distorted form and appearance. It felt as if I had sunk through the whole earth, and at the same time I experienced that my 'brilliant intelligence' had led me astray, had led me to a morbid stage of self-aggrandizement. In that moment, I lost all faith in my intelligence.

In this experience, I *saw* the animals, at least one of them. Shame in using my abilities in an egoistic way was my salvation.

On the threshold, there are forces and beings that hinder you from passing across without proper preparation. The dangers and destructive possibilities of using the separated soul forces are too great. If they are used without insight and humility, they can potentially destroy much, especially the will and the time-line forces. As mentioned, these forces are often described, in many different forms, as the *animals of the threshold*. To see and understand the three animals is one form of guardianship. These three animals are the pictorial representations of your feeling, thinking and will, and if you do see them, they don't look nice! Then you will understand that you have to work harder on your soul-properties before making a successful crossing of the threshold.

★

Later that year, a friend introduced me to an American writer called Carlos Castaneda. This was my first meeting with shamanism. After reading one of his books, I started to experiment with moving the independent parts around in my body before re-entering them with the 'I'. In this way, the number of possibilities multiplied greatly. It was then possible to divide my thinking from my feeling and will; to move this thinking part to my left hand and to then enter it with my 'I'. For example, I found at that time that if I looked through the thinking soul-part from my left hand, I could watch the mineral kingdom better, whereas if I looked from my right hand, the animal kingdom became clearer.

★

Testing out and struggling with spiritual experiences at the threshold was what filled parts of my youth, but my main occupation at this time was dealing with the normal problems of puberty. Plenty of such problems showed up. There was heart-pain, alcohol consumption and partying, as well as schoolwork, reading books and studying.

When I started to read my first spiritual books, I understood little of their content. They were too intellectual and too alien for me. At that time, I did not really understand that I often *was* in the spiritual world, and that I actually *had* abilities that none of my friends possessed.

At 17, I fell in love with a girl whose energy streams were in the form of a cross. As I have described earlier, such people are able to excarnate certain parts and thus enter the spiritual world. I felt this on an unconscious level, as I still did not believe in an objective existence of the spiritual world. At this time, I believed that my spirituality was just within myself as a subjective reality, but not as an objective reality. I was at that time what you might call an intellectual atheist, with a strong experience and love for God. Despite being an atheist, I read the Bible, and when I read about Christ, I often cried.

I knew the spiritual world, but I still did not believe in it. (Oh my God, what a schizophrenic situation!) So, when I met this girl, with whom I was 'with' for some months until she dumped me, I felt that, together with her, I was not alone in my experiences of the spiritual world; but I did not tell her about these experiences, as I habitually kept them all within myself, stupid as I was. So, when I finally had someone to share them with (to share something I did not believe in!), I did not tell her about my experiences. However, as a shy 17-year-old boy, I could never divulge these innermost thoughts, as I was too introverted. In addition, as a self-defined atheist and intellectual, I did not actually believe in this inner world of mine. I categorized it as 'just in my mind', and believed it had no real or objective existence.

Later I wrote this poem:

'... together with her
the heaven and the earth merged,
and the universal love
spread to all of the creation ...'

How tragic! I loved her so much; she was my whole soul and life; she was the door to my spiritual 'reality'; she was my everything. But she did not want me. She dumped me, and that almost cost me my life. At 190 cm tall, my weight plummeted from 72 kg to 62 kg in 6 months. That love almost killed me.

Finally, I had found a being with whom I could relate and converse, yet we were unable to do this, as I never made the first move in this direction. She treated me in a very hostile manner. I did not understand this then, but now I do. I loved her energy streams, the cross in her body, although later I understood that I did not actually love *her*; I loved her *ability* to enter the spiritual world, and to bring me there together with her, thus soothing my pain in being alone.

This is also an experience of the threshold: one may experience the utmost loneliness at the crossing, together with the yearning for some-body with whom to share it with.

Passing the threshold early in life is more difficult than later in life. However, in other respects it is better, as you then accept the changes more easily.

I did not understand this complicated attraction until, in 2014, I met Judith von Halle,[*] a German woman with the stigmata and a deep spiritual understanding. When I encountered her, I immediately saw that she also had this energetic cross through her body. Then I understood that it was these streams I had loved aged 17, and not the girl herself. In that moment, I was set free from that love which had burdened me for so many years.

Later in life, a female patient who I had been to school with told me that girls were afraid of me because they felt that I could see through them, which actually was the case.

*

Your own 'double', or doppelgänger, is also one of the guardians that push you back from the threshold. The double has been described by many writers throughout history: Jung, Novalis, Dostoevsky, Du Prel, Tieck, von Arnim, Brentano, Fouquet, Kerner, Poe, Hoffmann, Maupassant and Castaneda, to mention a few, and of course Rudolf Steiner. The book *A Picture of Dorian Grey* by Oscar Wilde accurately portrays the double.

This is a real being, with an existence apart from the human being, unlike the three animals. It is a non-physical, etheric being of the ahri-manic group of entities. It slips into our body just after we are born, and slips out again just before we die. This being has a deep relationship to our diseases, is fed by earth radiation (which I will describe later), and is connected to our negative karma. The doppelgänger can therefore be considered a mirror image of ourselves, apart from also being its own creature.

Just like there are three animals, and possibly a fourth time-line animal, there are also three or four doppelgängers on the threshold. We have:

---

[*]Judith von Halle was born in Berlin 1972. She is an architect by profession but has seldom worked as such. She felt herself to be especially bound to Christ since childhood. She encountered Anthroposophy in 1997 and worked part-time for the German Anthroposophical Society until 2005. From 2001 to 2003, she gave lectures on esoteric Judaism and the Apocalypse of St John. During Easter 2004, the stigmata of Christ appeared on her. Since then, she has only been able to consume water—that is, no solid nourishment.

- the already described ahrimanic double,
- the luciferic double,
- the karmic double,
- the electronic double.

To understand both the animals and the doubles—except for the ahrimanic double, which is a being of its own—we must comprehend that all our actions, in the life of thinking, feeling and will, create entities. These are creatures with a certain independent existence, as portrayed in Greek mythology by the Fates, in Norwegian mythology by the *Norns*, or the more modern descriptions of earth-radiation.

The electronic double is created by the electronic world that we have created. Since the advent of artificial intelligence, it is of utmost importance today that we understand it. The luciferic double is created from our feelings and the karmic double from our karmic actions.

Now we can see more clearly that we are not allowed to pass the threshold until we understand or know ourselves in a truthful way. This is why the first and foremost demand of any student involved with the Mystery Schools was, and will always be: '*O man, know yourself.*'. Even if we don't know ourselves to the utmost depths, we can still pass the threshold to a certain extent, as I consider the passing of the threshold a continuous process. The more you know yourself, the deeper you can go into the spiritual world.

The guardian of the threshold is usually a negative reflection of oneself, and in my experience, it was my shame that made me see him, and gave me a little more access to my threshold. Shame is a very important property of the soul: a judge of your own actions, and a regulator of the cosmos.

That moment of shame was my partial meeting with the guardian, and I passed the test. I refrained from using the power that my thinking could have given me, and stayed true to myself (just as Galadriel refrained from the Ring of Power in Tolkien's book *Lord of the Rings*, and remained herself).

This first guardian is called the Lesser Guardian of the Threshold, although it is manifold. Later, you meet the Greater Guardian of the Threshold, which many refer to as Christ. Then begins the work from the lower 'I' to the spiritual 'I', and ends with the Christ 'I', but that will be described later.

Before seeing the animals and accepting their ugliness, my passing of the threshold with the different soul-properties was, one may say, of a 'limited version'. I travelled to the borders of the spiritual world and a little beyond it, but not far inside it.

The acceptance of the animals is an important step in opening to the spiritual world. I met my first animal when I was 17, and the two others at the age of 40. However, not having met the animals in their totality, the spiritual world nevertheless opened more fully to me in my 21st year. At this time, I mastered to a certain degree the separation, the ability to follow in space the separate parts, the acceptance of the animals, and the change of thinking. This indicates that passing the threshold is a continuous process running throughout our lives. In this way, one could say that the threshold is endless, or that there are perhaps many thresholds.

This feeling of shame worked so deeply in me that I even *changed my way of thinking*. Before, I had thought in an intellectual way, but after this incident I started to think more in colourful pictures that—not being confined to the linear, crystalized structure of words—had no clear focus or conclusion, but instead gave a more holistic impression of what they contained. This aspect is important, and I want to describe it further.

This 'artistic' way of thinking, triggered by the deep shame I felt over my self-aggrandizement at the age of 16, took many years to develop, to become acquainted with, and to make accessible to friends—in short, to be able to communicate the pictures that were the foundation of my thought process. Before 16, I only thought in an intellectual way.

From the age of five, I experienced the ability to think, and as such the thoughts themselves could part from the rest of my soul. Even though they could part, they were still constructed of linear causes and effects, *pro et contra* arguments. Now, after feeling ashamed about them, they changed to more holistic pictures.

When I had to analyse a problem, increasingly I saw it as a colourful painting. Then I considered this painting artistically, trying to make it beautiful and balanced. If it was not, a solution to the problem had not been found. In that case, I might put a spot of red in a corner, and maybe some yellow, and then it became balanced. As a result, I could understand which argument or part of the problem this new red or yellow referred to, then translate this back to 'real life' and reach a conclusion. It was very difficult to translate this way of thinking to friends, or later to colleagues. A Swedish colleague (an MD) told me once that it had taken him 20 years to understand what I was saying. Actually, he said that it took *me* 20 years to translate my inner knowledge to words so that he, in turn, could understand me.

Another effect of this change in thinking was a loss of my earlier brilliant memory. In the early classes of primary school, I could remember a whole page and reproduce it in front of the teacher. Now, with this imaginative thinking, it was very difficult to remember. I must add that pure spiritual experiences beyond the threshold were even more difficult to remember. Memory seems to be dependent on the cooperation of the soul-powers, especially if the 'I' is not interfering too much.

In olden times (more than 10,000 years ago), the memory had enormous capacity, but it seems that this memory was mainly connected to the blood. Today, I experience the memory connected to the intertwined thinking, feeling, will and time.

When you pass the threshold and don't go back in time into the 'blood-memory', utilizing the memory becomes very difficult. After a purely spiritual experience (as will be described later), even if I see spiritual beings or actions in clear sight, afterwards the memory of it seems to fade away.

A short time after the experience with thinking and shame, I was ready to pass further into the land of the spirit, and I then had my first out-of-body experience. It was quite short and 'small', but for me it was just a beautiful experience. I woke up one morning and saw that everything was more radiant than usual. Everything seemed imbued with love and beautiful colours. I got out of bed and went to the window. It was a bright summer's morning. The colours, especially, were so unbelievingly full of life. Then I looked at my bed and saw that I was still lying in it. This unexpected shock brought me back into my body in a fraction of a second.

Other changes in thinking on passing the threshold

To observe one's own thinking is a difficult task, and often takes several years, or even a lifetime, to achieve. The pattern of thinking definitely changes during spiritual development. As these changes, at least in my case, have come quite abruptly and in a condensed form, they often create a considerable amount of misunderstanding, miscommunication and frustration, and it has been especially difficult to describe them.

Such changes in the pattern of thinking also demand new ways of performing habitual actions, down to a mundane activity such as playing chess. They also change the way I present myself, as if an entirely new side of my personality has revealed itself to me. During the attempts to establish this new personality, a disorder is created in the pre-existing thought patterns, and it is not easy to describe this.

There have been three such central changes to my thought patterns: at ages 6, 16 and 66 (interesting repetition of 6), and a minor one at the age of 62.

- The first change at age 6 was a transformation, from a mythical thought pattern to an intellectual thought pattern. This latter pattern was strictly linear. Later in life, I now consider this way of thinking as 'physical'.
- The second thought pattern, at the age of 16, was a change from a one-dimensional 'grey' cause-effect thought pattern to a two-dimensional thought pattern, consisting of colours. It was very much like seeing pictures, and reasoning or solving problems was like changing a colourful picture and watching if the balance and harmony within the picture became better or worse. This way of thinking was necessary for my spiritual development, especially within my work in healing and acupuncture. Later in life, I now consider this way of thinking as Imagination.
- The third change appeared at 62 years of age. This coincided with a deeper understanding of what the spiritual laws are, leading to the abandonment of all therapies that led to a translocation of diseases. Later in life, I now consider this way of thinking to be between Imagination and Inspiration.
- The fourth change in my thought patterns happened at age 66, and coincided with an understanding of the universal patterns within acupuncture, the loss of my ability to play chess. This is a three-dimensional thought pattern structure, as if I am within the picture described in stage 2. I am within the thinking itself, observing the cosmos or cosmic space from within, and not just observing it from without.* Now I consider this way of thinking as Inspiration.

At age 19, I started to attend the local agricultural college. I spent that year close to nature, learning how to grow vegetables. Here I met the concepts of biodynamic agriculture, but at that time I did not know that they originated in Rudolf Steiner's thinking and worldview.

At age 20, I started to study at the Norwegian School of Veterinary Science in Oslo. It was not easy to move from my hometown of Vestfold, with its nature and seashore, to the big city of Oslo. The big city almost killed me. I had to face a culture of drinking and seduction that was previously unknown to me, and I had no one to talk to about my spiritual

---

* These aspects will be discussed in Chapter 4, 'Senior Years' (after age 62).

experiences. Among the students and staff at the veterinary school, I faced the utmost and complete materialism and so became more and more desperate; I lost parts of my vision, developed a severe stress syndrome and eventually decided to quit my studies.

I told myself that if I did not find anything spiritual within one year, I would leave society in one way or another. In the summer, when I was aged 21, I felt I needed to leave the big city, and instead worked as a shepherd in the Norwegian mountains. There my meetings with the spiritual world started again, but now in a much more conscious way.

3. Adulthood

When I was 21, my spiritual work, experiences and further meetings with the threshold started again, just a few days after my 21st birthday, up in the beautiful valley of Gudbrandsdalen, Norway, at a place called Kvam. For the time being, I had quit my studies at the veterinary school because I could cope no longer with the materialism of modern science. In the middle of my first year of study, I had become deeply depressed and understood that I had to find the spirit, otherwise I would not survive.

I went to the bookstore and bought all books I could find with 'freedom' in the title, and then left Oslo and headed for Kvam. There, an old artist, a friend of my father, lived with her sheep and paintings. She was a woman with spiritual abilities: she could see ghosts and had several books written by a Norwegian-Indian guru called Sri Ananda Acharya. I started to work there, cared for the sheep, painted in the afternoon, and then walked in the mountains in the evenings and nights.

Then one evening, around 11 o'clock, something happened. I was walking along a narrow mountain trail when a small stone suddenly jumped over the path. I was shocked, and stopped. The shock loosened my soul and parted its soul-faculties, and suddenly the trees started to talk to me. I have described this at length in my book *Poplar*, and as the present book is more about crossing the threshold, I will not write here about the content of those conversations. This experience lasted for three days, during which time I had long and deep conversations with the trees.

In the present context, the most interesting thing to be learned from this three-day initiation into the life of trees is that the crossing of the threshold was induced by a small shock, which I received by seeing the stone 'jump' over the trail in front of me. When connections between one's soul-forces have been loosened, and the spiritual sense organs have been developed and activated, a little shock is often enough in order to pass the threshold.

This method of crossing over, by experiencing a little shock, has followed me for the rest of my life. Any minor or major shock pushes me over the threshold. When I was later called up to be a 'bomb shelter guard', I knew that a shock, such as a falling bomb, would have pushed me over the threshold. Then, I would have been of little value to the defence of the country, with the resultant inability even to lock the bomb shelter door!

Other shocks that have pushed me over the threshold have been: a sudden fear; watching happenings that seem to be impossible or unbelievable; keeping awake when wanting to be asleep; facing situations that could lead to death, or other 'jolting' experiences.

It is important to know that such shocks can also be created voluntarily. The main voluntary events that can cause the splitting of the soul faculties include the following:

- a small self-induced shock;
- an intense concentration on some external object like a tree, plant or creek;
- voluntary daydreaming;
- inducing a feeling of approaching death; and
- an important karmic meeting.

After a while, I started to get a certain control over the separation of soul parts, after which time I did not need jolts or shocks any more. I learned to control the separation with the help of my own consciousness and will.

I found the main techniques for splitting up the soul, in full consciousness, to be quite simple. First, I let some part of my soul or physical body *die or go to sleep*. Then *I enter with my 'I'* into this sleeping part, after which I let the 'dying' part 'flow out' (separately) in certain directions.

The directions are quite important.

- Going out with my thoughts into the cosmos, in an upward direction, at an angle of 45° to the horizontal.
- Going with my feelings—projecting them out into the wide expanses of the world—parallel with the horizontal.
- Going into other beings—especially animals that are suffering— with my feelings and co-experiencing their suffering.
- Letting one's will flow down into the earth, in a forward direction, at about 45°.

After my summer in the mountains, I had planned to work at a local institution for disabled people, a Camphill Village called Vidaråsen, based on the teachings of Rudolf Steiner, the father of anthroposophy. Little did I know what sort of place this was.

My second day at Vidaråsen, I happened to pass a bookshelf. I stopped and took out a book. The title was *Life between Death and Rebirth*. I almost fainted. What had I found? The leader of the village (Margit Engel) happened to pass by, and I asked her, 'Is what I read true?' She said, 'Yes, it is.' I stuttered: 'But do adults really have an interest in such things?' 'Yes', she said, quite plainly.

I was in shock, and totally excarnated. I passed the threshold immediately and conceived the huge universe of Rudolf Steiner in a kind of expanded view, as if I could see the whole cosmos.

Now, I started to delve into some of Steiner's books (he produced a totality of 100,000 pages of texts—written works and lectures—so of course I could only start gradually). Rudolf Steiner wrote about karma, life after death, the heavenly hierarchies, spiritual agriculture, spiritual medicine and many other important subjects that I have since been researching for many years.

Just two years later, I discovered the books of another great mystic, Edgar Cayce, whose transcribed readings also amount to more than 100,000 pages of the deepest spirituality, but of quite another kind to that of Steiner's.

I remember that while I was living there, I came down with a heavy cold and went to the local anthroposophical doctor (again Margit Engel) to get some help. She gave me some anthroposophical homeopathic medicines that she said should help with my cold. These medicines felt so holy and divine to me that I did not intend to use them at all, but kept them for 10 years, revering them as if they were holy objects.

In Steiner's work, I found many observations that coincided with what I myself had been experiencing, but also many that differed a little, although never totally. Some of the differences were the descriptions of the stages of passing the threshold, which had occurred to me in a different order than described in Steiner's writings.

However, this is not the subject of this book, and for now I will go deeper into my own experiences and techniques relating to the threshold—which of course changed somewhat after receiving this huge amount of knowledge presented by both Rudolf Steiner and Edgar Cayce.

I will now discuss in more depth:

- the separation of thinking, feeling, will and time, and their physical directions;
- how memory differs between the physical and spiritual worlds;
- activation of the twelve spiritual sense organs, along with the creation of the adversary counter-organs;
- meeting the four animals on the threshold (the ability of moral shame);

- the passing of the threshold itself;
- the immediate experiences beyond the threshold—the moving of the spirit;
- the spiritual apartments (the many 'rooms' in the House of the Father);
- Imagination—Inspiration—Intuition;
- death and rebirth;
- travelling in space and time;
- finding the twelve layers of the body, the sun/planetary system, the earth and the cosmos (zodiac);
- the reduction of the intellect;
- dark and white spiritual forces—evil and good, redemption and condemnation;
- the dark brotherhoods—the ill will of groups—the will to power;
- meeting other spiritual beings;
- losing abilities;
- the various doppelgängers, including the electronic one.

The separation of thinking, feeling, will and time

As described earlier, these separations happened to me involuntarily when I was a child. They appeared spontaneously until the age of 21, where-upon I started to control the process consciously. Between the ages of 21 and 33, I experienced both types of dividing, the voluntarily and the involuntarily.

At age 33, I decided that I no longer wanted the separation to happen spontaneously. With this decision, and a small needle in my ear, the ability disappeared with a huge explosion in my head, almost like a jet-plane flying straight through my skull, from left to right. From then on, I was on my own, and had to perform the separation out of my own conscious intention.

I then learned *how* to do this consciously, and the description below is of great importance.

To understand and describe the techniques of separating, I must first describe where the silver cord, that connects and controls the soul-fragments, is situated. The anchor-place of this cord is for me threefold, just as the soul is threefold, namely thinking, feeling and will, with the fourth addition of the time-line.

- For *thinking*, the silver cord is anchored in the brain. (We can find the physical anchoring of the 'I'-function in the area of the third eye.)

- For *feeling*, the silver cord is anchored in the four chambers of the heart. (We can find the physical anchoring of the 'I'-function in the heart.)
- For *will*, the silver cord is anchored in the warmth of the blood streaming through the limbs. (We can find the physical anchoring of the 'I'-function in the blood.)

In Buddhist meditation, some monks report that they reach Nirvana easier by cooling the blood of the limbs, which they achieve by sitting out in the cold. This clearly shows the difference between the pre-Christian method of passing the threshold and the post-Christian way, as Christ *is* the 'I', and the 'I' lives in the warmth of the blood. Nirvana is eternal bliss *without* the Christ, and I think this is a great danger for the present time.

So, when I travel into the spiritual world via my soul-fragments, I keep the connection via the silver cord, anchored either in my brain, blood or the chambers of the heart.

Concerning the heart, I can be more specific: in the heart chambers, we have four levels of 'I' consciousness, the lower 'I', the normal 'I', the higher 'I' and the Christ 'I', which I have found to be centred in the following chambers:

- the lower 'I' in the right front chamber;
- the normal 'I' in the right main chamber;
- the higher 'I' in the left front chamber; and
- the Christ 'I' in the left main chamber.

First, I have to be conscious of my will, feelings and thinking, and to be aware of the time aspect—in what year, day and time of life I am living. Then I concentrate on one of these abilities and imagine it in front of me, after which I let it fade away into the distance. Usually, I chose the thinking or the feeling. If it is the former, I let it 'fly away' at an angle of about 45° in an upward direction, and if it is the latter, I perceive it straight out, parallel to the ground. Also, I deliberately imagine that this ability is still connected to my body by means of a thin silver chord that is not straight, but goes, like a flowing current, between the loosening soul-abilities and either the third eye (thinking), the heart (feeling) or the lower abdomen (will).

After any one of these abilities is projected outwards, I always experience certain changes within myself. If *thinking* is projected out from the area of the third eye, my ability to think in an intelligent way is lessened. If I want to keep a grip on my intelligence as intellect, I need to pull my departed thinking back, but as long as the thinking stays outside, it is of no great intellectual value. However, some part of the thinking remains in the brain, as a connection to the projected part.

Thus, I experience two types of thinking on each side of the connecting silver cord. The thinking that remains in my brain is much simpler than the one that is projected outwards. It is a totally body-related intellectual thinking, while the thinking that is projected outwards is more like a living, flowing, cosmic thinking. My contact with the expelled thinking is through the silver cord, so when this connection is open, cosmic thoughts can be experienced, also in the remaining nucleus. It is also possible to follow the projected thinking through the silver cord and to experience the excarnated thinking directly, in its full glory. If cosmic thinking is experienced out in the cosmos without being experienced through the nucleus, the memory of this thinking wanes almost immediately, as explained earlier. When I observe cosmic thinking through the nucleus, it is possible to remember much more and to be conscious of the results of this thinking.

The effect of the cosmic part of thinking (without going through the nucleus) is a strongly joyful and light-filled experience, but without memory. The effect of thinking via the nucleus is a much calmer and darker experience. It is as if the periphery becomes a little darker and the landscape in front of me becomes somewhat pushed into a more violet or purple colour. Also, my vision gets a little tilted to the right, so I tend to hold my head at some $15°$ to the right in order to correlate with the tilted vision.

I have thus two options:

- I can stay in my body, just watching the thinking being outside, via the nucleus; or,
- I can go directly through the silver cord, into the translocated thinking.

If I choose the first option, I can watch the world from both inside the nucleus and the cosmic part via the nucleus. The thoughts then become a mix of both cosmic and earthly thinking.

If I choose the last option, I can watch the world from inside the separated thinking, and then the clear thoughts re-appear, not as my own, but as cosmic thoughts. With this separated thinking, I can watch hidden worlds, see through the earth and see through flesh (which is how I could always choose the black pawn when playing chess with my father).

It was in this way that I discovered that both the body and the earth have twelve layers (layers 9, 10, 11 and 12 are related to the heart, the eternal Mother, Sophia, and are in a state of continuous becoming). The eternal Mother expresses herself in the four chambers, which relate to the four 'I' qualities (lower, normal, higher and Christ 'I').

Also, there are twelve 'bodies' of our solar system (Sun, Mercury, Venus, Earth, Moon, Mars, Jupiter, Saturn, Uranus, Neptune, Pluto— plus the outer one beyond Pluto, which is not yet discovered) relating to both the twelve layers of the body, the twelve layers of the earth and the twelve zodiacal constellations.

As described above, when in the separation of a soul-fragment in thinking, I always feel this soul-ability split into two parts, the separated part leaving and the nucleus, or anchor-place, staying behind. In this separation, two main options are presented (with the possibility of several in-between variations), which are to stay with the 'I' in the parted fragment, or to stay in the remaining segment.

This description also fits the separation of the feeling (but not the will). In *feeling*, the main outpouring or port of separation is the heart. When the feeling is projected out from the heart towards the periphery, the feelings that are left as the nucleus change in the same way as the thinking: they get dull and grey. The fragment that departs seems to contain the better part of the feelings. These colourful feelings leave me, and as long as I stay or remain in the body, I experience only the dull and grey feelings. These remaining feelings are of a calmer and quieter variety. It is as if the etheric counterpart of the feelings remains in the form of the nucleus and that the astral part has left.

Between the remaining and the expelled feelings, there is a silver cord. Through this cord, I can travel with the 'I' from the nucleus to the expelled part and then choose where I want to stay. If I stay in the nucleus, I stay outside the cosmos. If I transpose my 'I' consciousness through the silver cord into the transposed or separated feelings, I can use these outer feelings as a sense organ for the entire cosmos. I often use this technique to diagnose patients who are a long distance away. With the translocated feeling, I am able to come into contact with all sentient beings of the cosmos. With the thinking, I am able to come into contact with the more material structures of the cosmos, like the earth.

The effect of feeling in the cosmic part, without going through the nucleus, is a strong, joyful and light-filled experience, but *without* memory. Feeling via the nucleus is a much calmer and also darker experience. It is as if the surroundings, the periphery, becomes a little colder. This feeling is *with* memory.

As in thinking, in feeling I also have two options:

- I can stay in my heart, feeling both inside the heart and/or in the cosmos, connected via the silver cord.
- I can go directly through the silver cord into the translocated feeling.

If I choose the first option, I can use my feeling heart as a sense organ from both inside the nucleus and the cosmic part via the nucleus. Then the feeling observations are a blend of the cosmic and earthly feeling heart.

If I choose the last option, I can watch the world from inside the separated feeling. Then, the bright and joyous aspect of cosmic feeling appears, not as my own, but as cosmic feelings. This cosmic feeling is much brighter and more colourful, similar to my experience of colours when I went out of my body for the first time aged 16.

If my *will* is projected out from the lower abdomen towards the interior of the earth, I first feel this separation as a certain loss of my will. I feel unable to do anything. As with the thinking and feeling, there is still a remaining nucleus of the will that I can operate autonomously. In will, the experience of both the excarnated fragment and the remaining nucleus is somewhat different from both thinking and feeling. The main difference is that I have difficulties in observing both the material world and the spiritual cosmos through the will. I use will almost exclusively in *acting*, in *doing* some deed, in either the material or the spiritual world.

I use the effect of the will in the following way: When the will has separated down into the lower part of the abdomen, then into the legs, into the feet and even into the earth, I lose much of the ability to act (as with both thinking and feeling). However, as soon as I let the will flow upwards again, this inability will change into its opposite. When, on its upward-flowing path, the will has reached the area of the abdomen, I meet it with a strong and intention-filled thought. In this mixed 'will-thought', the willpower then creates a force that flows out into the arms, the legs or into some other living entity in the outside world. This force can give strength to the arms, the legs, or influence any outside living being. If I direct this force to an acupuncture point, this point will then be treated. If I direct it to some earth radiation, I can move this radiation or change it in some way.

With this force, we can influence many aspects of ourselves or others, perform physical tasks with great power, such as correcting a misaligned hip or neck, hit a tennis ball at great speed or play a perfect tune on a flute.

According to Rudolf Steiner, humanity collectively passed the threshold during the twentieth century. To my mind, this means that the separation of thinking, feeling and will is happening more or less to everybody. This can lead to many strange experiences, even to frightening and inexplicable depressions or similar psychic conditions. Some spiritual scientists think that this will lead to an increasing incidence of psychiatric epidemics. The only way out of this is to *understand* what is happening, but this will be difficult as materialistic medical science—especially psychiatry—today denies the existence of the spiritual world.

Remembering

My experience with the girl when I was aged 16, and the consequent shame and change in my thinking, also brought about a loss of much of my ability to remember. Remembering is dependent on the time-line, on thinking being attached to feeling, and also to what you have done with your will. The wholeness and integration of these four soul abilities is the foundation of remembering. When the bonds between them are severed, remembering becomes difficult. After a spiritual experience, you seem to forget it all, as if it never happened. This may be difficult to accept, and sceptics may scoff. Still, it is so.

The activation of the spiritual sense organs

These supersensible sense organs were being prepared as early as prehistoric times. They have been developing as part of our evolution, especially during the last two millennia. However, today there has been a dangerous development, which I will discuss below briefly, as it definitely relates to the passing of the threshold.

Rudolf Steiner described thoroughly the existence of twelve senses.[*] He claimed that each of these faculties acts as portals to the physical, etheric and astral aspects of both man and the cosmos in which we live. Each sense is connected to one of the divine beings of the first hierarchy, expressed in each of the twelve signs of the zodiac. In this way, they can be viewed as a twelvefold entity, also connected to the twelve layers of the body and the earth, as well as the twelve planets.

In Steiner's description of the human being, he categorizes our make-up from several perspectives. First, he divides us into four layers, consisting of our physical, etheric, astral and 'I' sheaths. However, if one also

---

[*] Rudolf Steiner, *The Twelve Human Senses*, lecture in Berlin, 20 June 1916.

considers our spiritual future as including the higher levels called Budhi, Manas and Atma, this concept of a fourfold being can be seen from a different perspective as having both seven, or even nine, levels.

Ultimately, a primary trinity of the powerful soul-faculties of thinking, feeling and will governs our higher selves, as well as all of creation, the cosmic counterpart of which is found in the Trinity beyond the zodiacal circle. They represent the fundamental processes by which our cosmos is organized and developed, and weave themselves into all aspects of creation. This trinity encompasses the entire cosmos, the divine angelic hierarchies, as well as the sub-natural world of spiritual beings such as elves, 'hidden people' and other elementals.

This latter aspect of our universe can be seen with the spiritual eye as an 'upside-down' reality of the physical world (or perhaps it could be our world that is upside down!). In this way, one can imagine that our feet were to make contact with their reverse image beneath the spiritual earth.

The three cosmic forces play a role in every aspect of our lives. They are revealed within the anthroposophical medical system as the three fundamental poles of:

- the nerve-sensory system (thinking);
- the rhythmic system (feeling);
- the metabolic/muscular/skeletal system (will).[*]

However, it is of paramount importance that we understand that this template can also be applied to the twelve senses, particularly when we are considering the steps toward spiritual initiation known as Imagination, Inspiration and Intuition:

- Imagination (the four physical senses of touch, life, movement and orientation);
- Inspiration (the four soul senses of smell, taste, temperature and sight);
- Intuition (the four spiritual senses of hearing, speech, thought and perception of the 'I' of others).

The senses described by Steiner are extremely complex formations, as they exhibit both an outward and inward direction of flow. For example, the eyes which perceive the cosmos send an outward etheric stream, enabling them to receive also an inward flow of information from what they are viewing. It is a general spiritual rule that any

[*]Rudolf Steiner and Ita Wegman, *Extending Practical Medicine*, Rudolf Steiner Press 2000.

movement automatically creates a counter-movement, even in the case of time.

The twelve senses are also present in the luciferic, ahrimanic and human karmic doppelgängers. These three entities employ the senses in a unique way. The human karmic doppelgänger uses the physical sense organs as we use them in the material world; however, the ahrimanic and luciferic doppelgängers create their own mirror images of these structures. The templates that ahrimanic forces utilize are situated deeper within the physical body, while the luciferic templates are more superficial, infiltrating the astral sheath. For example, in the eye, the ahrimanic sense organ lies about one cm behind the material optical structure, whereas the luciferic organ is in front of the eye. I perceive the ahrimanic organ clairvoyantly as a greyish structure, similar to a tin plate.

I would conjecture that most people believe that the explosion of technological advances has heralded an era of great progress. With the push of a few buttons, anything and everything can be found, researched, bought and sold. In addition, our ability to connect immediately with one another through social media has morphed the concept of the written word. Language has now taken on a divisiveness of monumental proportions, as the 'instant word' has assumed the role of becoming the most effective weapon since the invention of the gun.

Therefore, it is no wonder that the existence of electronic technology has also created an effective tool for the blossoming of adversarial forces. Below, I explain the exact methodology by which Ahriman, as the primary sinister force, can manipulate these technological devices in order to gain control over the future of humanity. His[*] major access point is through the portals created by our sense organs.

These ahrimanic sense organs are also activated and developed through the viewing of electronic screens. From this, it can be surmised that there are actually three aspects to each of these sense organs. If one considers all twelve sense organs and combines the fact that all these senses are employed by three doppelgängers (including ourselves), and that each organ is involved in both an outgoing and an ingoing stream, we can conclude that we are actually dealing with 72 qualities that must be considered when understanding sensory function. Note that all twelve senses can make a spiritual observation, especially after a separation of the feeling, thinking, will and time-line. The ultimate danger is if the

---

[*] I often use the term 'his' for Ahriman and Lucifer although these two forces or entities actually have no gender.

adversaries have developed the eye or other sense organs further than the 'clean and good' spiritual sense organs. Then we could possibly be deceived by the ahrimanic or luciferic worlds and be lost to the spiritual development intended for us.

The first sense organ I will discuss is the eye, the foundation of sight and also central in the use of imagination and clairvoyance. Regarding the eye as a physical organ, I have observed that when viewing a living object, especially in nature, the inhabitants of higher spiritual hierarchies also share one's observation. I have also found that the sense organs with little or no fat, such as the eye, have a stronger affinity to the etheric; however, when one is observing the screen of a mobile phone, the observations are intertwined with another reality, in which colours diminish and ahrimanic forces dominate.

Regarding Lucifer's and Ahriman's effects on our sense organ of sight—whether we are observing the results of these demonic influences on the nature of the physical world, or on the sub-nature of the virtual electronic world—I find that both demons can thrive on the latter, including the internet, artificial light, LED displays, computer monitors and mobile phones. Paul Emberson describes this in his book, *From Gondishapur to Silicon Valley*.

Because the adversaries such as Lucifer and Ahriman are able to take part in this underworld via electronic technology, handwriting is a safer alternative for communication, as it is under the domain of the angelic realm.

The strength of the aforementioned doppelgängers is woven into the sensory observations. Paul Emberson claims that the use of computers stimulates the adversarial forces' strong hold on our existence. For example, if one views a movie, then this actually strengthens the ahrimanic doppelgänger's visual sense organ. This ahrimanic eye is grey and large, similar in appearance to a plate made of tin. In 1917, Steiner addressed his concerns about attending the cinema.[*] He described that the eyes of those watching a movie take on the sense organs of Ahriman.

An interesting reference to such an eye in literature can be found in

---

[*] Rudolf Steiner, *Cosmic and Human Metamorphoses*, lecture 4, 1917: 'While people are sitting at the cinema, what they see there does not make its way into the ordinary faculty of perception; it enters a deeper, more material stratum than we usually employ for our perception. A man becomes etherically goggle-eyed at the cinema; he develops eyes like those of a seal, only much larger, I mean larger etherically. This works in a materializing way, not only upon what he has in his consciousness, but also upon its deepest sub-consciousness.'

Henrik Ibsen's play *Peer Gynt*. There, the trolls' eyes are described as 'plates made of tin'. Also, the King of the Mountain Hall wants Peer to marry his daughter (i.e. marry the ahrimanic world), and he wants Peer to undertake minor surgery—a slit in the eye. Peer can then be hoodwinked by the adversaries into thinking that everything he sees in the ahrimanic world is beautiful, and therefore assure his marriage to the Troll King's ugly daughter. This shows that Henrik Ibsen was aware of the ahrimanic plan to conquer the eye, in order to prevent humanity seeing the real spiritual world. Today this plan is being carried out quickly and efficiently throughout the world by the ubiquitous use of electronic media.

The second sense I would like to discuss is that of feeling. The related organ to this sense at the physical level is the skin. My observations regarding this organ date back to well before my understanding of anthroposophy.

During the first years of my veterinary studies at Oslo University, I spent some time between classes observing people, especially those who were overweight. I saw, with my spiritual eye, that many of these people had their stomach paunch extending beyond the etheric sheath. The fatty tissue was in a sense hanging loose, out of the etheric field. In this way, the effect of the sense organ that allowed *clairsentience* was diminished. In other words, being overweight can have a negative effect on supra-sensory feeling. Therefore, when a person goes on a weight reduction programme, it may be possible to redevelop the spiritual sense of touch as the etheric sheath expands in an outward direction, thus diminishing the stranglehold of Ahriman and Lucifer on this particular sense organ.[*]

To understand this, we should look at how Rudolf Steiner described clairvoyance as a relationship between the physical body, etheric body and astral body, especially when the spiritual bodies are outside the physical form. For example, during the time of Atlantis, the etheric sheath of the head extended beyond its physical counterpart. In this way, Atlanteans were clairvoyant and able to observe the etheric world. However, if the outer border of the etheric body is behind the skin of the physical body, the supersensible sense organs become muted. Therefore, it appears that the ahrimanic and luciferic sense organs develop in pro-portion to our growing love of technology, especially over the past twenty years.

Just as Goethe wrote that the sun creates the need for human eyes, so

---

[*] This might be why Christ fasted as he resisted the temptations of Lucifer and Ahriman during his 40 days in the desert.

will the existence of virtual media and electronic devices create the need for an ahrimanic eye. I have observed that children are very quickly developing a special affinity for understanding such devices, as the doppelgängers' eyes become more sophisticated. The healthy spiritual forces, in contrast, avoid such devices that create a dissolution of healthy social connections among people.

An even more sinister connotation created by this dissolution, lies in the inability of advancing our goal toward spiritual initiation through the process of Imagination, Inspiration and Intuition. Therefore, we should proceed with caution to limit electronic communications in our daily life by reducing the use of email, Facebook and similar forms of social media.

Our soul life, etheric life and our physical bodies depend on our will to control the use of electronic media. We must protect our future now, for our children and for the future of the spirit of humanity as a whole.

The meeting of the four animals on the threshold

This is the meeting with your everyday, earthbound thinking, feeling and will, plus the 'illusion of time' as a fourth animal. Our thinking, feeling, will and conception of time are far from being as perfect as we think, and our pride and belief in our own soul abilities greatly hinder our passing of the threshold. That is why we meet them just before we reach the threshold—or at the threshold itself. If we don't understand and accept that these ugly, fractured and inadequate beings are our own soul abilities of thinking, feeling, time-observation and will, the passing of the threshold will be dangerous and almost impossible. This is why the Guardian of the Threshold refuses entry until you have understood the deeper meaning of the animals, in order to protect you from the adversarial forces, which will have easy access to your soul if you don't understand their significance.

At the moment of meeting the four animals, if you are honest, you will realize the inadequacy of your proud intellect, your feeling life and power of will. In addition, you will realize that you have been lying to yourself about these matters, fearing the spiritual world and hating its claim on you to be honest and true. In this moment, you realize the importance of developing your *love, hope and faith* in order to withstand the ugly and disastrous aspects of yourself. You also realize that the distance created between yourself and the real spiritual world through the adversary phenomena of lying, deceit, fear and hatred also create the illusion of time that you experience as the fourth animal. Thus,

- lying—counteracted by truth;
- hating—counteracted by love;
- fearing—counteracted by courage;
- distancing—counteracted by breaking the illusion of time.

The first time I saw the inadequacy of my thinking was during the incident with the girl when I was aged 16. This was my meeting with the first animal, the one representing thinking, which Rudolf Steiner described as the 'third animal of the threshold'. Then I felt shame.

The next stage of seeing or meeting the animals happened to me in Ireland, totally unexpectedly, as often happens in these cases. To understand this meeting, it is important to know that the animals can be met from two different directions.

- They can be encountered from this side of the threshold, due to work and meditation.
- They can be experienced from the other side of the threshold, due to grace.

The Irish experience was, among other things, also a meeting of the three remaining animals, but this time from the other side of the threshold. When I was on the other side, the spiritual forces protected me; I was in 'grace'.

Whilst travelling in Ireland at a junction on the road from Galloway to Dublin, two gnomes or leprechauns stopped me and pointed very vigorously in the direction they wanted me to travel, north via Longford (actually they pointed in the opposite direction, but in the etheric world everything is supposed to be seen as in a mirror, or in reverse). It was almost as if they were in the physical world; they seemed to be as material as the ground on which they trotted. I followed their advice, knowing from previous experiences that when I saw leprechauns in such 'physical reality', they brought very important messages.

I travelled in the northeastern direction towards Longford. The landscape in this area was typically Irish, with small rolling turf-covered hills, clusters of trees, stone houses, abandoned farmsteads and the occasional modern house dotted about in the surrounding area. Cows were grazing, the sky was blue and all was quiet.

After about 90 minutes of driving, just before I came to Longford, I spotted that grass was on fire on the left side of the road, about 200 metres away. The flames were high and fierce, and it seemed as if the fire was out of control. I stopped the car in a small space on the right side of the road, rolled down the window and looked out.

Again, something unexpected happened. The flames shot up in the air, changed direction and came directly towards the car. They entered through the open window and made a spiralling movement around me, encircling my head and upper body. I was not burned and nor did I feel any discomfort; I only experienced a strange feeling of being invaded by something. I was immediately transported to another realm of existence. But for how long I was gone, I do not know.

Where was I? I was transported to the upper or higher spiritual world. There I experienced how my thinking, feeling and will should have been. I was in a state of complete and total communication with the entire cosmos, on all levels:

- My *thoughts* were crystal clear, understanding everything.
- My *feelings* were completely transparent, encompassing all and everything in a love so deep and warm that I never thought was possible.
- My *will* was as if I could reach the highest mountaintop and overcome the most difficult task.

I *was* the entire cosmos. I was one with God.

Eventually I came out of this experience, and slipped back into the ordinary world. Exhilarated and dazed at the totality of such a cosmic experience, the ordinary world felt so dull, so grey, so disappointing and so very depressing. I then understood and experienced how my thinking, feeling and will could or should have been, and how these soul-faculties were distorted and transformed into the three terrifying animals that Rudolf Steiner describes so graphically.

I then *saw* the three animals. Then I felt *depression*.

The passing of the threshold itself

From my experience, this threshold is no deep canyon or high wall or anything resembling an abyss. It is a gradual journey of many steps, with many different experiences and many different problems. These experiences require one to be brave, and to keep faith in the good powers and the wise guidance of karma.

According to spiritual tradition, there are seven main levels in the passing of the threshold. One of these is losing all footing in the material world, called the 'Trial by Air'.

The most difficult experience I had was this 'losing of everything'. This three-year experience almost physically killed me. I lost everything, or so it seemed, on the experience of this downward journey. First, I lost my lover, then my children, then my friends, then Nature, then the stars.

At this point, I will explain this 'losing of the stars' more specifically, so that it becomes clearer to the reader. At this stage of descent, when I had lost everything, I comforted myself that I at least had the stars; that at the very least I could look up to the stars and find comfort in not being absolutely alone.

I felt relieved for a few days, until the terrible consciousness rose in my brain, that the light from the stars had been travelling towards me for maybe thousands of years, and that the whole firmament might by now be gone, might be dead. This realization took me into a further descent. After two and a half years of this death process, I simultaneously suffered from heat stroke, pneumonia and severe diarrhoea after lecturing in Florida for some weeks in August.

Today I remember little from this time. I fainted from just walking up the stairs. I felt as if I was dying; that my life was slipping away. In this death-like situation, the last thing I could own were my own feelings, and even these left me. Hallucinating, I saw them floating outside me as three coloured balloons, red, blue and yellow (as the three animals have these colours, perhaps this was spiritual sight and not a actual hallucination).

I had lost everything. Then a certain stiffness in my body overtook me, resembling rigor mortis. I was sure I was dying. This hardening lasted for some weeks, and then suddenly it all turned. I slowly returned to life, and after a year I felt good again. This experience is part of the passing of the threshold: the losing of the material world, and maybe, at times, your soul and your sanity too.

Very early on the pathway to the spiritual world, many seekers will meet the phenomenon of the *poltergeist*. I still do not know why I had to experience these phenomena and nobody I have met truly understands them either. They may be linked to the aspect of 'loosening', and possibly prepare one for this unexpected loss of everything.

The poltergeist is an unseen power or entity that takes things away from you or plays tricks of dematerialization that may be unpleasant, but could be useful for others. I have never seen this *Geist* as an entity with either my physical, etheric or astral eyes, and neither has anybody else I know.

I will tell of two such occasions to illustrate the meaninglessness (or in some cases wisdom) of their actions, but as mentioned, such actions may pull one out of the material realm, which is important in the passing of the threshold.

The first experience happened at Vidaråsen, the Camphill village I lived in for six months. I was told to wear a suit for the Bible evening that was held every Saturday. As I had no suit, I borrowed one from my father. Coming into my little room with the suit, I laid it carefully on the bed. I looked away for two seconds and when I looked back it was gone—it disappeared, never to show up again. Who knows, maybe another person suddenly was given this suit, one who needed it dearly.

The next incident I will describe is when my wife and I were in Amsterdam. We had the day free, and placed our luggage in a locker at the central station. I inserted the money, and received a coded ticket from the machine. I then took the ticket and handed it to my wife. In the moment of passing the ticket from my hand to hers, something happened, but at that point neither of us realized. I thought she took it, and she thought I took it back.

Coming back to the locker in the afternoon, we could not find the ticket. We searched our pockets and belongings ten times, quarrelling about who had it. Getting the locker opened involved a lot of difficulty, but after half an hour and the help of several guards, we managed to get the suitcases out and did not miss the plane. When coming home, opening the front door and walking into the front room of our house, there, in the middle of the table, lay the ticket, untouched and without a single crease!

The immediate experiences beyond the threshold

When we pass the threshold, we might meet many interesting characters, reminiscent of *Alice in Wonderland*. These entities follow other rules, laws and logic than those we have in the physical world. The laws in the etheric realm are often totally opposite to the ones we have in our physical world.

For instance, we meet the elementals, which appear very differently on different continents of the world:

- huge elementals called 'trolls' and tiny elementals called 'flower elves';
- dead people, souls stuck in time, standing in one place for 1,000 years;
- the Hidden People and the high elves;
- demonic, even satanic beings.

As I understand from others, the first area or experience from the land beyond is the astral world; however, for me, the etheric realm was the first area of the spiritual world I entered after passing the threshold. These two worlds or realms of the spiritual are quite different from each other.

Why this has happened to me in a reverse order I do not know, but it illustrates how different our personal paths into the spiritual world can be.

Beyond the threshold we can enter different kinds of worlds:

- the etheric world;
- the astral world;
- the angelic world;
- the demonic world;
- the elemental world.

As a small child, I first met the *etheric* world unconsciously. Then, when I was 21-years-old, a few weeks after my birthday I re-met the etheric world consciously.

Streaming lines of etheric energy, infused with personality, intent, power and direction, characterize the etheric world. I experience this world best in nature, especially amongst trees. I see the strong weaving etheric lines, almost as snakes between the trunks. These lines are close to the earth in winter and higher up in the summer. They are alive, they are conscious, but not in the way we humans are conscious; rather, more in a non-egoistic, plantlike way.

The flowing etheric within these moving 'snakes' goes in two directions, to the left and to the right. The stream to the left goes towards the past, and the stream to the right goes to the future. If I step into these streams with my body, standing with my feet in the middle of the snakes, I can actually let myself be taken by the stream and experience the past. That is, if I let myself be taken to the left. Then I can stand there in some wood, between the trees, and float or drift in time. I see the old formations of earth, crystals and leaves relating to the trees. If I use the tree-etheric to travel in time, I do not experience human or animal history, only the history of the trees.[*]

In puberty, I unconsciously met the *astral* world, but many years later, at the age of 50, I encountered it consciously. It is especially in the spring and early summer that one may experience the astral world as it shows itself in nature. This world lies just beyond the threshold, although for me it is found a little further behind the etheric realm. I experience the etheric world in shades of grey, whereas the astral world

---

[*] I have written about this in my book *Poplar*.

is full of colours, twinkling and bright. In the realm of trees, this world is to be seen hovering above the etheric world, further from the forest-floor.

The first glimpses I had of the *angelic* world appeared during my experience in Ireland, when I found myself in this world for about half an hour. However, the main experience at that time was the meeting of the feeling- and will-animals on my return into the physical world. The angelic world was for many years a hidden realm for me. During most of my life, I have met elemental beings of many kinds: I have met demonic beings; I have seen the depths of the earth and alien planets. I even believe I met Jesus (in distinction to Christ) once—but the angelic world was still a closed realm.

Quite recently, this realm has started to open up, but just a little. This opening to the angelic realm did not happen until I reached the age of 66, at which point I had worked through an important part of my old karma.[*] Then I was able to open my heart to the angelic world.

I started to meet the *demonic* world at the age of 25, due to my medical training at the veterinary college which involved the killing of animals (which we had to perform in order to become veterinarians). These killings were often performed without first sedating the animals. I once had to cut the throats of rats using blunt scissors, without any sedating substances. This reminds me of the training of the Nazi aspirants in black magic, where they were given small birds and needles and had to inflict the most pain, for the longest possible time, without killing the poor creatures. The optimum pain in the longest possible time was the goal. This is the usual training in black magic, used throughout the centuries by the followers of Klingsor.[†]

Later, I came across 'real' demons in the street, in the forest and in the desert. As a therapist, I most often saw the demons residing in the sick bodies of humans and animals. The demons I meet in sick people or animals are of two types, the luciferic, astral ones and the ahrimanic, etheric ones. I always perceive the astral demons in the head region and the etheric demons in the region of the belly, as caudal.[‡]

Between these two types of demons, we will always find the Christ

---

[*] Described in my book *The Forgotten Mysteries of Atlantis.*

[†] Klingsor is the name of the black magician in both Wolfram von Eschenbach's *Parzival* and Wagner's opera *Parsifal*. Rudolf Steiner stated that he had been a historical figure who lived in Sicily.

[‡] Situated more toward the cauda, or tail, than some specified reference point; away from the head.

Force and are thus able to perceive the angelic realm. Thus, not far away from the threshold—actually on the threshold itself—reaching both into the physical, astral and the etheric world, lies this demonic world.[*]

The dark brotherhoods

After becoming accustomed to the darker forces, I started to meet groups of people that used these forces to gain power. I was led to such people when I was on the other side of the threshold. They are actually quite easy to spot. 'Normal' people or humans have a characteristic lemniscatic etheric circulation. The etheric body is large, like a vertical figure eight (8). People that have easy access to the spiritual world often have a cross-like form in their etheric body, as if they have already met Christ in the etheric, which they actually may well have.

People who are engaged in antichristian activities have two characteristics: they have a big, dark void in their chest, sometimes extended also to their face, and they may have an opposite cross pattern, with the cross point around the knees.

Meeting the *elemental* world is another experience just beyond the threshold. In this world we meet all the elemental beings that live there: elves, gnomes, water-spirits (undines), wind-spirits (sylphs), the hidden people,[†] dwarfs, goblins, gnomes, salamanders, trolls, *hulders*[‡] and many others. After I was 21 years of age, I met most of these elementals consciously.

Shamans and other nature healers often deal with and see this world, but in my opinion, this is a world in which we should tread very carefully. The elemental entities have no morals and exchanges with such entities will seldom turn out to be of benefit.

---

[*] This reaching into the physical world needs a further comment, one which seems to be ignored and overlooked by so-called New Age people today. The good spiritual entities have to conform to a cosmic law which does not allow them to interfere with human freedom. The dark forces are not subject to this cosmic law, and can enter our physical world as much as they desire. This can be seen in the phenomenon of the crop circles found in southern England (they can actually to be found all over the world, but not as much as in Wiltshire).

[†] Hidden people or *Huldufólk* is an Icelandic euphemism for the elves, as their folklore says you should never call them by their actual name.

[‡] A *hulder* is a seductive forest creature found in Scandinavian folklore.

The spiritual apartments

After passing the threshold we enter, more or less involuntarily, into individually different 'levels' or 'rooms'. It is stated in the Bible that 'my father's house has many rooms', and it is very important to be aware of this. When we pass the threshold, we enter the 'room' relating or fitting to our level of knowledge and consciousness.

If we have realized a certain truth and attained a certain level of understanding, this will bring us to another and more fitting room. This new 'room' will also bring with it the necessary way of thinking, attuned to our new level, which also means that we will lose certain abilities, thought patterns or activities that we had before which no longer vibrate at the correct level of our new room. This change is reflected throughout our whole existence, not only beyond the threshold, but also in our everyday life, sleep and work.

In many fairytales, we have the story of the poor boy who finds a large castle wherein he meets a princess. There are many rooms in the castle, and the boy is allowed to look in every room but one. Of course, he feels compelled to look in this forbidden room, and when he does, the whole castle disappears and he is left with nothing. There are many secrets in such a fairytale, but the one relating to this theme, of many spiritual compartments and of entering a new room that changes your whole reality, is important to understand.

The most interesting and illustrative experience I had in this connection is the following: I was pondering deeply why the effect I had in curing cancer differed so much when using either a 5-, 7- or 12-element structure in acupuncture therapy.* I had just realized that the Yellow Emperor, who was the founder of the important acupuncture theory of the five elements, was the incarnation of Lucifer himself. This realization came to me in a flash, and had and will have huge influence on my professional work as an acupuncturist. Rudolf Steiner has stated that this incarnation of Lucifer occurred in China in 2,500 BC. The use of five elements in acupuncture treatment allows the luciferic, demonic elementals to translocate into other beings, and not to transform. The dark (or light) lord has thus fooled us for 4,500 years.

This realization catapulted me into another room in the spiritual world, and my thinking changed in a blink of an eye. In this new compartment, logical thinking was even more alien than the new compartment I had

---

* This is explained further in Chapter 4.

been pushed into at the age of 16. In this new way of thinking, earthly logic became even more alien, to the point at which playing chess was made almost impossible. Before this, I was a relatively good chess player, but during the space of a single day, I lost most of my understanding and ability to play. Thankfully, I simultaneously lost my great interest in playing chess!

Travelling in space and time

The ability to travel in space and time happened for the first time when I was 16-years-old. That was a one-off experience, and this ability reappeared only when I was 21, during my stay at Vidaråsen. In all such 'travels', I have seen that they never happen by chance, or just for 'fun'. There was always a deeper meaning that usually showed itself many years later, and had important implications at that later time.

Whilst at Vidaråsen, one day I sat in the hay and separated my soul-fragments. On this day, the fragments separated more easily and wider apart than usual. This led to the 'I' leaving my body through my eyes and floating upwards. I passed through the whole planetary realm: I saw the Moon, Mars, Jupiter, Saturn, Uranus, Neptune, Pluto and also one more planet outside Pluto. This had important implications in developing my twelve-element system, that 45 years later threw Lucifer out of my cancer treatment. I had a hard job coming back.

Another time I was in Oslo Cathedral, in which I had been baptised when I was seven-months-old. I was baptised very late, as my father was an atheist and my mother had to smuggle me to Oslo to baptise me. The second time I visited this church was 25 years later, as a student living in Oslo with my young wife and new born child. I was tired, hungry and exhausted as I walked into the church one evening at the end of December. I sat down to rest and immediately separated my soul-faculties. This time they separated more than usual, and I watched in amazement that all the people sitting around me changed into beings that seemed to be made of dust. They dissolved into dust. Then I automatically entered the time-line and time started to travel backwards.

I sat with open and amazed eyes, watching history in a backward-playing film, displaying knights, old farmers, warriors of old and numerous historical happenings. Time reeled backwards, faster and faster, and after about half an hour I could see dinosaurs walking around me. I actually sat there with my physical eyes open and saw all this. I had never travelled that far back in time before, and just as I felt that I was about to lose the connection with and through the silver cord, I started to feel a little uneasiness, almost a certain fear of not finding my way home again. I actually considered what it would be like to be forsaken in this 'lost world', with many dinosaurs and no other humans to speak to. The thought was not attractive to me at all! After about half an hour, I managed to reunite with my physical body, and suddenly I could see the other people in the church.

Another time I travelled in space to witness a person in great sorrow and need. I was of course unable to do anything at that time, but several years later I met this person again in real life, and was then in a position to help. This opened my eyes to the existence of karma, for how else on that first meeting could I know my help was needed 10 years later?

★

After working with the etheric streams that flow between trees, I found a safer and better way to work with time: the time-line, the time-spiral and the double time-stream.

I often walked in the forest in 2007, as at that time (between 2004 and 2011) I owned a 600 dekar* farm in Ramnes, Norway. I regularly watched the streaming etheric, snake-like flowing forms that moved between the trees. I can only describe them as some kind of living matrix weaving between the trees—actually between all entities—which almost includes the whole world. They are like dark snake-like streams of water, all having a different power and thickness. This living matrix of different black snakes, interwoven into all of nature, included the farms I passed by, the trees, and everything that was alive. I saw how these power lines streamed from the woods, embracing barns with cows, pigsties and houses. They went from tree to tree and between people and trees. They were stronger between trees belonging to the same species, between animals of the same species and between humans.

Wherever there were animals, the contact was both stronger and larger than where there were no animals. Maybe this is the reason we feel so connected with animals and nature. We feel as if we are part of a greater correlation, a part of something bigger, which of course we are. This experience made me aware that the entire Creation is woven together in one grandiose cosmic togetherness, and if something changes or dis-

---

* 1 dekar = 1000 m².

appears, it will affect all of us. If one thing in this entirety suffers, the whole of the cosmos will suffer.

When the sun shines on the trees, the centre of the streaming energy—the tree energy—is about two thirds of the tree height from the ground and focused towards the sun. At night, the centre is one third from the ground and focused downwards towards the earth. Therefore, as I am on the ground, I feel contact with this ethereal world much better during night-time, or when in the shadows. The spruce trees do not pay so much attention to the moon. At night, they communicate more with each other and with me if I am there.

When I rode out in the woods one day, I became almost jealous of Balder, my horse. His communication with the trees was about ten times stronger than mine. It seems as if plant-eating animals are much closer to the ether-streams of the plants and trees than we humans. There are many claims that horses can 'feel' the plants they eat, i.e. which ones are poisonous and which are beneficial; however, if a plant has lost its ether-streams as in the case of hay, it is dead, and the horse no longer feels what is poisonous or not.

The communication between trees and skiers or joggers is the same as the one they have with me, only that people running or skiing do not pay attention. They somehow block it out. It is sad to see so many people training by means of jogging in the forest today, and so few keeping fit by walking.

Twelve layers of the body, solar system, cosmos and Earth

When working with separating soul-fragments over many years, I discovered in 2001 that the body also consisted of twelve layers, the ninth, tenth, eleventh and twelfth relating to the heart and to 'I' consciousness. Standing on the top of the Atlas Mountains on 1 January, when the veil between the physical and the spiritual worlds is at its thinnest (during the twelve holy days and nights), I clearly saw that there were twelve layers in the Earth, the innermost four layers relating to the development of the 'I' and the Sophianic mother. This is not yet fully acknowledged or understood.

From travelling through space, I found that there are twelve celestial bodies in our solar system, the twelfth not yet found (Sun, Mercury, Venus, Earth, Moon, Mars, Jupiter, Saturn, Uranus, Neptune, Pluto, and then one more). I already knew, of course, that there were twelve celestial zodiacal constellations.

Below I will describe the twelve layers of the body in brief, and relate them to the twelve layers of the earth and to the influences of the demonic realms.

	Layers of the body (according to Thoresen)	Layers of the earth (according to Rudolf Steiner)
First layer	The astral sheath of the body	The physical earth
Second layer	The astral and the physical body	Fluid earth, high pressure, expansion
Third layer	The physical body. If the physical is turned into spirit, it shows the opposite. If a spiritual entity points to one direction, it means the other way.*	*Damp (or air) earth.* Here the substances are in a damp state. This layer is full of life and wants to expand even more than the second layer. It is closely connected to passions in the human and animal world, and the entire level is filled with living streams of strong passions. One peculiarity is that here all the emotions are changed into their opposite: love into hate and so on. Typical of luciferic actions.
Fourth layer	The parasitic bodies within our physical body and alien physical/etheric entities (bacteria) that we use to digest foodstuffs. Alien bodies also exchange DNA with us, as they are involved in physical development.	Water earth or form-earth. Here, all substances are in an astral form. The astral form is the negative of the material form, just as in Devachan. These astral forms are the source of our astral development.
Fifth layer	I. The etheric body, warmth ether (infra-red). Also, the scars of the body, both physical and mental, that have come from life's experiences of living in the warmth.	Fruit earth, where everything is pure life. Everything is living here. This is the blueprint of all life, but in an inverted form.

---

*Regarding this, see further in my book *The Forgotten Mysteries of Atlantis*, 2015.

Sixth layer	II. The etheric body, light ether (blue = Ahriman, red = Lucifer). The scars of the body, both physical and mental that have come from life, from living in the light.	Fire earth, which is in direct contact with human emotions, especially 'fiery' emotions. Human suffering will upset this layer and lead to volcanic activity. 'Dragon-energies' can be found here. Balrogs.* Related to the magnetic field of the earth, and by such to Lucifer and earthquakes.
Seventh layer	III. The etheric body, chemical-ether (ultra-violet). Production of vitamin D. The scars of the body, both physical and mental that have come from life, from living in sounds and/or substances.	Mirroring earth or reflecting earth. Here are found all the natural forces and laws used within physics, but as their opposite. All moral impulses are here changed into their opposite. All colours appear in their complementary form (all ethers are here changed into their opposites).
Eighth layer	IV. The etheric body, life ether (green). The scars of the body, both physical and mental, that have come from life, from living in the life forces.	Splintering earth (layer of numbers, according to Pythagoras). All living entities are here splintered into multiple 'copies' of their original. The source of black magic. All good qualities are transformed into the opposite (like Seventh layer). Origin of all evil in the world.
Ninth layer	The demonic 'I', the lower 'I'. The lower passions that we are aware of. Ill will. To be transformed in the future.	The core of the earth. Here is the origin of black magic. This layer resembles both the human brain and the human heart. It contains the demonic 'I', the lower 'I'.
Tenth layer	The 'I', the ego, egoism. The 'normal' self. To be transformed in the future, with the help of Christ / Sophia to Manas.	(According to Thoresen, not Steiner:) The 'I', the ego, egoism, which may be transformed through the development of man into a good form of the 'I'.

---

*Balrogs are fiery demonic creatures in J. R. R. Tolkien's Middle-Earth legendarium.

Eleventh layer	The higher 'I', idealism. What we call the superego. To be transformed in the future, with the help of Christ/Sophia to Budhi.	(According to Thoresen, not Steiner:) The higher 'I', idealism which may be transformed through the development of man into a good form of the 'I'.
Twelfth layer	The Christ-'I', Divine Consciousness, Christ Consciousness. Will be transformed in the future, with the help of Christ / Sophia to Atma, Spirit Man.	(According to Thoresen, not Steiner:) The Christ 'I', the divine consciousness, Christ-Consciousness, that may be transformed through the development of man into a good and angelic form of the 'I' (which will lift humans to the Tenth hierarchy of angels).

Imagination—Inspiration—Intuition

The first impressions I had when initially entering the spiritual world were mere fleeting streams of etheric power. Gradually, the elemental spirits emerged, followed by the astral colours and demonic entities. In the beginning, this was in the form of floating images with no understandable meaning. This is called *imaginative* consciousness or Imagination.

After 25 years, the meaning of the pictures, of the Imaginations, started to appear. When I saw an Imagination—and this Imagination may have been a mental picture or an etheric entity, even a creature of the elemental world—I immediately knew what the picture meant, understood what the entity said, or comprehended what the gnome signalled.

For example, one day, when I saw a date appear as a picture/Imagination around the head of my acupuncture teacher, I immediately knew that this was the date of his death, and sure enough he later died exactly on that date. Or, when a huge sea-elemental (*draugen**) showed up before my boat (it looked totally material), I knew that it predicted my death, and turned around immediately and headed back to land. It later proved that should I have continued my boat-trip, I would have drowned. This is called *inspirative* consciousness or Inspiration.

---

* The *draugen* or *draugr* in Norse mythology is the ghost of a man who has drowned at sea. He appears in the form of a terrifying, screaming monster to seafarers and tries to drown them.

After 30 more years, a further change emerged in my experience of the spiritual world. At this time the imaginative pictures, the entities or spiritual happenings no longer appeared as outer, understandable images. Now, I not only understood their meaning, but I saw the world from 'inside' them, experiencing their inner life. This is called *intuitive* clairvoyance or Intuition.

I will explain about how to train these three different kinds of consciousness in Chapter 5.

Remembering spiritual experiences

Memory in the physical world is dependent on the connection between thinking, feeling, will and the time-line. When these connections are broken, memory, as we know it here in the physical world—at least in our time—is no longer possible. It is very difficult to remember spiritual experiences, both in the spiritual or in the physical world where you find yourself as soon as you re-enter everyday existence.

I remember spiritual experiences in the following way: Immediately after the spiritual encounter, I repeat the experience in the 'normal world', in my head, as memory pictures, and in this way imprint it in my normal memory. Thus, the memory of all my spiritual experiences is actually the memory of the memory.

As we can now see, the passing of memory from the spiritual world to the physical world is difficult; however, the opposite direction is quite different. In the spiritual world, it is possible to remember everything that was experienced in the physical world.

One time when I passed the threshold, I entered a state of mind or 'room' in the spiritual world where everything that I had experienced, every word that I had read or written, was standing in complete clarity in front of me. I could remember *everything*. This room did not feel like the so-called 'akashic records', which are like an immense photographic film that has recorded all our *actions* during all of our lives. The room I had entered contained all I had read, seen, thought and written, and was more like a record of pure knowledge, rather than actions as recorded in the akashic chronicles. The remembrance of all *knowledge* was like a special sub-room within the main room of the akashic records.

During the first three days after death, which is also a passing of the threshold, one sees or experiences the whole of one's life pass by in powerful pictures. The time-line here is in the opposite direction. What one registers here is more the *intentions* behind the actions that have been committed, not what we may call pure remembering.

Pure remembrance is linked to the etheric/physical bodies. Intentions are linked to the etheric/astral bodies.

According to Steiner, after death one will later re-experience all that has happened during life, but this time seen from the standpoint of 'the other', i.e. the person who experienced the result of your actions.

Meeting spiritual beings that help you

We will also meet many spiritual helpers before, at and after passing the threshold. They may be guardian angels, elementals, initiates or higher spiritual beings. Some even meet Jesus himself as a guide, and that brings about a reassuring feeling that nothing bad can happen. I myself have met such helpers several times.

My experience at the threshold has often been met with resistance. By this I mean I was not welcomed by the demonic entities. I understand this resistance was a result of my particular karma. Nevertheless, I still experienced crucial help at important moments on the path.

Example 1

The small sunbeam that hit my neck: This was one very important experience during my first year at veterinary school. I could not understand the ugliness of the world, all the suffering, and one day, in deep depression, I took a walk in the forest north of Oslo. The day was grey, cold and snowy. At a certain moment, there was a small rift in the clouds, and a tiny sunbeam appeared through them. This sunbeam hit me on my neck, and in a split second I received the mighty love of the sun. I felt that this love was for all human beings, even for the most miserable ones, and this filled me with great joy and pleasure. The deep and lasting depressions that I had suffered throughout my life until that point now disappeared forever, never to return.

Example 2

The singing tree-plants: This was a very life-giving experience, when I needed it most. This also happened during my first year in veterinary school, and as indicated earlier, this schooling was not very uplifting due to all the suffering and killing of animals. One day I passed an area of small spruce plants, and suddenly one of the small plants began to sing for me. I stopped, and then the neighbouring one started to sing, then another. Soon all the small plants were singing in a giant choir and the joy this gave me lasted for many years, even until today.

Example 3

The three men in black: This happened when I slept in the very room (called Oscar's Gate) where Rudolf Steiner had given many of his lectures, including those on 'the Fifth Gospel', when he visited Christiania (now called Oslo). In the middle of the night, I woke up totally alert and awake. Two metres away from me stood three men, all dressed in black from head to foot, discussing me and my life. I instantly and intuitively understood that these three men were Rudolf Steiner, Christian Rosenkreutz and the Master Jesus. This experience gave me life-long assurance that I was on the right path.

Example 4

A Sophianic experience in Ireland: This was when I was allowed to experience the ultimate joy and force of cosmic thinking, feeling and will. (This has already been described in the section on the three animals at the threshold.) This experience was twofold. First, I experienced the might of spiritual thinking, feeling and will, and then, on my return to the physical world, the ugliness of the three animals—the earthly feeling, thinking and will.

Example 5

The 'hand' saving my life at sea: This is described in my book Demons and Healing. *The story is about how a huge sea-elemental (Draugen) saved my life from drowning.*

Example 6

Meeting Jesus in Israel, during my first visit to the country: He appeared first as a material man, although dressed in a traditional outfit with sandals, long hair and a long nail on his left little finger. Jesus has been by my side ever since that meeting.

Losing material things, memory and/or different abilities

The losing of memories when passing back over the threshold is described in Greek mythology as 'drinking the waters of Lethe'. Every time I have passed further over the threshold, I have gained further knowledge or understanding. At the same time, I have always lost some abilities:

- When seeing the third animal (thinking) at the age of 16, I lost part of my intellectual and logical, linear thinking.
- When, aged 21, I suddenly understood that my ability to see through flesh was a spiritual ability and not an 'ordinary' physical one, I lost that ability for a few years.

- When I understood that my healing of cancer was due to and dependent upon the translocation of pathological entities, I immediately lost the ability to cure cancer for four years.
- When I understood that the whole five-element system used in acupuncture was designed by Lucifer himself, in order to allow his obedient workers to translocate, I immediately lost all ability to play chess (more about this in Chapter 4). For me, this indicates that the thinking process within chess is based on the same foundations as the luciferic deception.

4. Senior Years (62–)

The most important and interesting experiences that have happened, and still are happening after the age of 62, are to do with my long struggle of many years to cure cancer. When I treat a cancer patient, I always cross the threshold in order to diagnose and treat this disastrous but highly spiritual disease. What I will describe in this chapter is centred around two main experiences:

- Firstly, the fact that my long-used cancer treatment suddenly stopped working in 2014.
- Secondly, that during one single day in 2018, it started working again.

These two seemingly impossible happenings are of far-reaching importance for our understanding of the threshold and the spiritual world beyond, as we shall see.

Additionally, two important findings or realizations emerged during this time:

- The importance of the 'Middle Point'.
- The possibility of splitting/dividing Lucifer and Ahriman in both the vertical direction (opening to the angelic realm) and the horizontal direction (opening to the archangelic realm).

To be able to explain the very important insights that I gained from my struggle to cure cancer, I will briefly describe the development of my cancer treatment.

My journey towards understanding the nature of cancer began in 1983. I realized at that time that cancer had to be treated differently from other disease processes. The solution seemed both simple and profound. Using the principles of five-element acupuncture, I saw cancer simply as an extreme excess of a normal fundamental process. Therefore, the organ controlling the cancerous organ must be deficient, or lacking control. My conclusion was to strengthen the deficient organ and regain control over the excessive and cancerous organ. I called this method 'the controlling treatment'. I believed at that time that this was a superior treatment, and I was under the misguided belief that this might have held the key to curing cancer for the future. And for several years, the results seemed to prove my theory.

Between 1984 and 2014, I treated more than 1,000 patients, both animals and humans, suffering from all kinds of cancer. The results were particularly good; however, I had seen for many years that most methods of treating diseases with acupuncture actually enforced a *translocation* of the disease to other people and/or animals (actually almost all diseases in animals are translocated from their owners in a 'natural' way, but the traditional alternative treatment enforces this system).

If one reviews the literature of various alternative medical systems, there are revelations that show this translocation phenomena was already being observed by some of the great physicians of homeopathy, such as Dr Constantine Hering,[*] the author of Hering's Laws of Cure.[†]

In March 2014, I decided to try to do something about this translocation, in other words to try to stop it, and instead to develop a method to transform the pathological demons. It was at first only a decision, yet this mere intention caused a rapid decrease in the effectiveness of my cancer treatment. At about the same time, the effectiveness of the treatment also decreased for most of the students practicing my cancer treatment method, without them knowing anything of the loss of effectiveness of my treatment.

Finally, in late 2017, I began making headway towards a solution to this dilemma.

I understood that the real problem of translocation was hidden in the five-element thinking of the Chinese[‡] medical system.

---

[*] Dr Constantine Hering MD (1800–1880). Hering is aptly called the 'Father of Homeopathy' in America. Originally a sceptic, he was convinced of homeopathy's efficacy after an objective study of its principles. He went on to expound upon the 'laws of cure'.

[†] Hering's Law of Cure states:
- Cure occurs from above and downwards. It progresses from the head towards the lower trunk, that is to say, the head symptoms clear first. With regard to the extremities, cure spreads from shoulder to fingers, or hips to toes.
- Cure occurs from within outwards and progresses from more important organs (e.g. liver, endocrine system) to less important organs (e.g. joints). That is to say, the function of vital organs is restored before those less important to life. The end result of this externalization of disease is often the production of a 'treatment cutaneous rash'.
- Symptoms appear in reverse chronological order. More recent symptoms and pathology will clear before the old; the disease 'backtracks' so to speak.

[‡] In understanding and changing this terrible error that the five-element thinking represents within alternative medicine and acupuncture, I feel I have a special obligation and karmic duty to put it right, as I believe that I myself, in an earlier incarnation 4,000 years ago, was complicit in incorporating this teaching into Chinese culture, 500 years after its introduction by the Yellow Emperor himself.

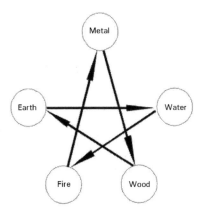

I then considered the four-element thinking of the Greeks, the six-element thinking of the Middle East, the seven-element thinking found in anthroposophy and finally the twelve-element thinking found in astrology.

Here it is necessary to give a short explanation in relation to the term 'element', as it may confuse the reader. I am not referring to the classic elements as found in Greek philosophy, but more to the cycles of function, or groups of function, that we find in nature.

Man is a microcosm relating to and mirroring the great macrocosm. The Chinese observed in nature how the different elements worked together, and created the sequence of the five elements. The Greeks did the same with their four elements. We must then look to nature and see where we can find other groups or families of similar function. Where in nature do we find systems other than the fivefold? This demands a new way of seeing.

Anthroposophy is a spiritual science inspired by integrative thinkers and scientists, such as Johann Wolfgang von Goethe, Rudolf Steiner and Kurt Goldstein. Using this philosophy allows us to develop ways of perception that integrate self-reflective and critical thought, imagination and careful, detailed observation of the phenomena.

According to these principles, the organism teaches us about itself, revealing its characteristics and its interconnectedness with the world that sustains it. This way of approaching science enhances our sense of responsibility for nature. As Goethe states, all of nature's individual aspects are interconnected and interdependent: all the parts of an individual have a direct effect on one another—a relationship to each other—thereby constantly renewing the circle of life. We are thus justified in considering every creature to be physiologically perfect.

By understanding these tenets, I finally understood that I had to transform the *perceptions* of a pre-Christian system (the law of the five elements) to a post-Christian system, based on anthroposophy. Maybe I could use the Goethean observations of the cosmos and its inhabitants, for which anthroposophy is so well known. The most important and fundamental concept in anthroposophy is:

- the threefold division of man;
- the sevenfold division of time;
- the twelvefold division of space.

I theorized that it would be possible to make two new systems based on these divisions. I also experimented with the so-called 'Middle Point' (described later) and the six-elements, as used in Jewish culture. During my search, I gradually discovered that each acupuncture technique that I modified resulted in different effects on my patients, as shown below:

- In the five-element system of Chinese acupuncture, translocation seems to dominate.
- In the six-element method, suppression seems to dominate.
- In the seven-element method, transformation seems to dominate.
- In the twelve-element method, transformation seems to dominate.
- Stimulating the Middle Point in a single patient, the spiritual disease resolves, but the physical pathology remains.
- Stimulating the Middle Point in a circle of patients, higher spiritual beings become involved and seem to help create a deeper and karmic spiritual healing amongst the entire group, but physical pathology remains.

Description of the six-element system

This system was discovered during my search for a transformative solution in cancer treatment, but it did not work in a transformative way; rather more as a suppressive. I will therefore not spend much time here in describing this system.[*] However, it will illustrate that the results of any treatment can vary greatly, according to the worldview of the therapist or the originator of the system. This insight will be very important when we later view the deeper foundations of the five-element system.

---

[*] For more on this see my book *Demons and Healing*, page 115.

Description of the seven-element system

In anthroposophy, the concept of astronomy reaches far beyond the material concept of the universe that we have been taught by science. The planets to which Steiner refers represent much more than the material rock and gaseous formations we observe through our telescopes; they represent real spiritual beings. What we are also unable to observe directly is that these planets also represent different phases of the evolution of the entire universe, including ourselves.

Therefore, according to anthroposophy, at the beginning of time the solar system was in a planetary phase called Old Saturn. So far, there have been four incarnations of our system: Old Saturn, Old Sun, Old Moon and the Present Earth that we inhabit. Our current planet is a culmination of the previous stages of cosmic evolution, as part of the continued evolution of the entire solar system. Between each phase of evolution, there is a death or a pause, followed by a reincarnation into a new form.

After the present Earth stage of evolution, the cosmos will dissolve, then rest, after which everything in the solar system will reincarnate in a new condition called Future Jupiter. This process of creation, dissolution and rest will be repeated in two more phases: Future Venus and Future Vulcan.

We relate the spatial relationship of the seven planets and evolutionary stages to the seven main organs. These relationships are recorded in several ancient texts and are shown below:

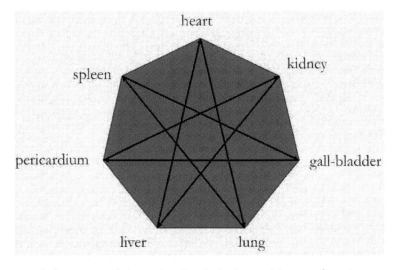

Body processes relating to time (cosmic development) in a star formation

- Sun: heart (HT)
- Moon: reproductive organs (PC)
- Mercury: intestines, lung (LU, LI, SI)
- Venus: kidney (KI)
- Mars: gallbladder (GB)
- Jupiter: liver (LV or LR)
- Saturn: spleen (SP)

This represents a total of seven planetary phases and seven organ systems, instead of the five or six organ-meridian systems dealt with by the Chinese and the Jews.

Description of the twelve-element system[*]

We relate the spatial relationship of the twelve zodiacal constellations to the twelve meridian processes of Traditional Chinese Medicine. These

------

[*] Some interesting details about the twelve-element system: If we look carefully at the structure of the twelve-pointed star, we will soon realize an interesting geometric pattern. The structure actually consists of three crosses, each formed as a double cross:

- The first cross consists of the axis of the BL to LI and LU to KI, crossed with the horizontal axis of SP to GB and LV to ST. All the diagonals in this cross are as acupuncture Yin-Yang pairs.
- The second cross consists of the axis of the SI to the BL and the KI to the HT, crossed with the horizontal axis of GB to PC and TH to LV. All the diagonals in this cross are also Yin-Yang pairs within acupuncture.
- The third cross consists of the axis SP-SI and HT-ST, crossed with the horizontal axis of PC-LU and LI-TH. All the diagonals in this third cross are again Yin-Yang pairs within acupuncture.

I am uncertain how to explain or deal with these relationships at this present stage in my research.

The circle of fifths and the anticlockwise chromatic circle that appear in the twelve-element zodiacal transformative system: For many years, I have studied the relationship between the twelve tones in our musical scale and the zodiacal constellations. Likewise, the relationship between the acupuncture meridians and the musical tones are rather interesting. When we have put up the zodiacal signs in a circle (see illustration), they will be in the following succession: Libra—Scorpio—Sagittarius—Capricorn—Aquarius—Pisces—Aries—Taurus—Gemini—Cancer—Leo—Virgo. If we then add the relating meridians to this succession we get the following line: LU—PC—GB—SP—SI—BL—LI—TH—LV—ST—HT—KI. We also see from the figure of the twelve signs that the controlling star is related to the interval of the fifth. We see for example that LU is controlling BL, then the related tones will be C and G, which constitute a perfect fifth, and so it is with all the meridians and tones. Also, it is worthwhile to observe that if we follow the notes counterclockwise, we get the chromatic scale of C—C#—D—D#—E—F—F#—G—G#—A—A#—B and again C. Extraordinarily interesting indeed!

relationships are recorded in several ancient texts, modified by myself, and are shown below:

- Aries: large Intestine (LI)
- Taurus: hormonal system (TH)
- Gemini: liver (LV, LR)
- Cancer: stomach (ST)
- Leo: gallbladder (GB)
- Virgo: heart (HT)
- Libra: lungs (LU)
- Scorpio: sexual organs (PC)
- Sagittarius: gallbladder (GB)
- Capricorn: spleen (SP)
- Aquarius: small intestine (SI)
- Pisces: bladder (BL)

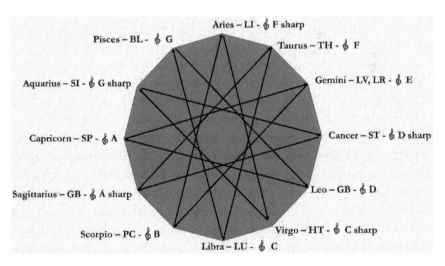

12 elements in transforming cycle, after Thoresen

Up to this point, my descriptions have been preliminary. Now we come to the really interesting material (both the disappearance of the effect in 2014 and the loss of my chess-playing ability in 2018).

- My insight into translocation and my intention to rectify this resulted in the inefficacy of my cancer treatment, although not of any of my other treatments. This teaches us that when we have the strong intention to try to change something that the spiritual powers have decided, they change the rules of the game. We must then be aware, on or beyond the threshold, that any change we might make will have far-reaching consequences. Others have found this too, for example Dirk Kruse, who describes the changes that the crossing of the threshold made in his life. The lecture he gave about this was titled 'Between Suicide and Madness' *(Zwischen Selbstmord und Wahnsinn)*, as he found the changes very hard to adjust to. My intention to change the results of my cancer treatment also changed the effects of the old medical procedure for a whole group of therapists (my students).

- My insight that the five-elements treatment was a cause of translocation resulted in my total loss of ability to play chess. This teaches us the same thing as does the 2014 incident, namely that all additional insight and will to change something, results in an often-unexpected change in the 'room' where this change occurs.

To understand this insight better, let me describe my realizations about the five-elements: *In whose interest* is it that almost all acupuncturists in the world use the five-elemental thinking, causing translocation of the luciferic elements in disease, especially in cancer?

Margaret Fleming DVM researched the historic texts mentioned below and writes:[*]

The first mention of the five elements extended as far back as the earliest records of Chinese history, nearly 3,000 years ago. At that time, it was stated that it is a way to describe natural processes that were hidden from our view, the latter being a definition rather reminiscent of the spiritual world. A text from the *Zuo Zhuan* refers to the elements as being formed by 'officials' who are presented as spirits or deities and who require offerings to be made to them.

The Tibetan shamanistic religion, Bon, also embraced the five-element philosophy, but referred to the phases as experiential sensations of the natural world. According to this religion, the elemental processes are fundamental metaphors for working with external, internal, and secret energetic forces and believe they are all aspects of a primordial energy. Their scriptures also state that the five elements reflect successive phases in our becoming human beings. Throughout these phases, our experience is shown as God-like, with intensities of illumination and with each element having a distinct bright, light-filled colour.

---

[*] See *Spiritual Medicine* by Are Thoresen DVM and Margaret Mary Fleming DVM, CreateSpace 2018.

As time passed, the spiritual connotations of the five elements as a way for someone to respect the universe and the order of things as an upright moral being were minimised, and the emphasis was placed on it as a medical system. This occurred in the Han dynasty when Daoist notions of immortality were held.

By the first century BC, the *Huangdi Neijing* (The Yellow Emperor's Inner Classic) became the premier textbook regarding Huang-Lao (Yellow Emperor Laozi) Daoism. In this work, the subject of acupuncture and Chinese Medicine is elaborated. Here the emphasis is placed on the concept of the body being a microcosm of the universe.

The Yellow Emperor appeared in the ancient texts in approximately 2,700 BC. Most scholars agree that he was first described as the 'God of Light'. Historians claim he was descended from *Shangdi*, the primordial deity in the Shang Dynasty. In addition, according to Sarah Allen, an expert on this subject, he was originally an unnamed being, referred to as 'the Lord of the Underworld' and was depicted as a dragon. His mother, Fubao, was a virgin who, through an immaculate conception, conceived him after being hit by a lightning bolt.

To continue the thread that he was perceived as a spiritual being, folklore has recounted an event when he visited the mythical East Sea and met a talking beast. This beast taught him the knowledge of all supernatural creatures. Also called the 'Yellow Deity with Four Faces', he represents the centre of the universe and by regulating the heart within, he brings order without. It is written that he said, in order to reign, one must reduce oneself, abandoning emotions. Huang Di went into the wilderness to Mt. Bowang to find himself. It is said that at this point he created a void where the forces of creation gathered that made him more powerful. He imparted the concept that the centre (similar to the middle) is also the vital point in the microcosm that is man, and that this centre is where the internal universe is described as an altar.

He further elaborated on the idea that the body is a universe saying that by going into himself and incorporating the structure of the universe, he would gain access to the gates of heaven.

Finally, he is also seen as a manifestation of the divine order encased in a physical reality that can open to immortality. These statements are similar to the life of Jesus during the incarnation of Christ, complete with a virgin birth, a temptation in the wilderness and the promise of eternal life. Thus, the implication is that he is a reincarnation of a higher spiritual being. But what being could he be?

Rudolf Steiner delivered a lecture[*] on November 4, 1919 in Dornach, Switzerland, in which he told the story of three of the most important incarnations of high spiritual beings that have and will shape the destiny of all of humankind. How we develop as selfless spiritual beings, and how we cope with the lessons, gifts, and challenges that these three powerful figures bestow upon us will determine the fate of humanity. These three spiritual beings are:

- Lucifer
- Christ
- Ahriman

Steiner tells us that our human soul contains a powerful seed of primeval wisdom, but from the beginning, this had to be nurtured to achieve the capacities we needed to attain to become developed beings in a material existence. We needed a spiritual guide from the higher hierarchies to assist us in the growth of our I consciousness. This teacher was the fallen archangel Lucifer. Steiner estimated his incarnation to have occurred around 3,000 BC in East Asia. In the previous paragraphs, we have researched the ancient archives regarding the story of the Yellow Emperor, Huangdi, and have shown that he was born at the same time and in the same region. It is thus logical to assume that the body that received the incarnation of the light bearer was none other than this being. For those of us practising the ancient art of Traditional Chinese Medicine, particularly five-element acupuncture, this historical correlation is of paramount importance.

This might be the first clue why the five-element cancer protocol not only became ineffective, but also may have never been a truly transformational approach. It appears to me that these concepts, which employ a luciferic impulse despite their alluring nature, are ultimately outdated and even dangerous tools. They must now be replaced by a higher impulse that came 3,000 years later through the impulse of the second incarnation, that of Christ.

Lucifer, as Huangdi, brought us the world of thought and speech, the characteristics necessary to develop our I through a pagan wisdom. This wisdom could be only obtained from luciferic sources and the initiates of the time were obligated to receive it without becoming tainted by the ulterior motives of the light bearer, which are to

---

[*] Lecture 3 in the cycle *The Influences of Lucifer and Ahriman*, SteinerBooks 1976.

abandon the path of Earth evolution, in order to win humanity for a kingdom alien to that of Christ.

As has been stated earlier, the gifts of Lucifer are a unification of man, spiritual inspiration and creativity. After all, Lucifer lures us away from our intended path with a brighter light. However, the lure of materiality is always there to swing our consciousness towards the other side of the pendulum, leading to a disdain of the spiritual, replacing it with a kind of stark rigidity, and towards the third future incarnation, that of Ahriman. According to Steiner, he will incarnate in the West, before 3,000 years after the incarnation of Christ have passed.

The tendency to split up into groups and to form different nations and different languages, creating greed and dissent, gives fodder for the development of an ahrimanic impulse. This impulse is characterized by a hatred of spiritual science and the ease of being simply given a kind of false gift of clairvoyance in the future. Without a counterbalance, humanity will succumb to his rigid, cold and ossified kingdom on earth, with no hope of complete spiritual evolution.

This counterbalance of the Christ impulse must be nurtured now, during this epoch. In this way, Christ will be able to stand between the two adversaries who can bestow their positive traits to our education and advancement, but be kept at bay by the balancing power of Christ standing in the middle. Therefore, it is our responsibility, as it is of all of humankind, not to allow Ahriman to overwhelm us with materialism.

Steiner felt that the main tool to combat Ahriman is the application of the philosophy of spiritual science. Any luciferic methodology will create a bypass around Christ allowing both adversaries to join hands and destroy all hope of our spiritual redemption. Thus, our task is to focus all our efforts towards employing those tools that facilitate the evolution of man towards reunification with the Saturn primal energy and eventually to become part of the hierarchy of spiritual beings. Real wisdom has to be obtained, not from ahrimanic complacency, but from struggle through sacrifice and pain. For in this struggle, we prevent the rigidification of our world and allow the warmth of the Christ impulse to return to infuse future Vulcan. Therefore, humans are balanced between Lucifer and Ahriman, and Christ is our wingman leading us away from the ending battle with Lucifer to engage in the future battle against Ahriman.

Finally, concerning treatment, Steiner discusses the importance of numerology in this equation. He felt that the old pagan ways were reflected in the pentagon and the number five, which is considered a symbol for Lucifer. Therefore, when we engage the five-element system in treatment, we are actually strengthening Lucifer and counteracting the Christ impulse. The hexagon, however, reflects the number six, symbolizing the power of Ahriman. Therefore, using the hexagon in acupuncture, for example, fast-forwards us to the world of Ahriman. Our spiritual evolution, however, is achieved by the use of the number seven, reflected in the seven planetary phases and the twelve zodiacal constellations.

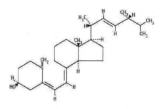

Molecular structure of vitamin D (see further in Addendum 2)

The Middle Point method

I discovered this method by studying the works of Judith Von Halle. She stated that a diseased patient should be healed using 'Christ Consciousness'. After looking carefully at 'the Group' sculpture by Rudolf Steiner depicting Christ standing between these two pathological entities, I realized that the healthy energy of the Christ consciousness lies between these yin and yang structures residing in the body. I named the locus that could accomplish this task: the 'Middle Point'. This Middle Point is situated in close connection with the heart, in between the abdominal ahrimanic structure and the luciferic structure situated close to the throat. This Middle Point can be awakened by means of a touch or some other physical stimulus in this area, and also by the application of a directed conscious thought, either one-to-one or in a circle of people.*

A new way of separating and passing the threshold into the angelic realm

Working with the Middle Point in the treatment of different diseases, painful conditions and cancer, led me to a closer understanding of its meaning, and consequently is of great importance to the writing of this book about the threshold.

After working with the separation of luciferic and ahrimanic demons in

---

*Awakening the Christ Point or Middle Point in a circle of people, in my experience, is of the greatest importance. I have described this method and its implications in detail in the last third of my book *Spiritual Medicine*. The effect of the circle is in itself a dividing of the three soul-forces: thinking, feeling and will.

patients for almost five years (both individually and within the circle of people mentioned), alongside separating my own soul-fragments to enable me to pass the threshold, I finally realized it must also be possible to pass the threshold by separating the luciferic and ahrimanic demons in myself. As described earlier, the part (or 'room') of the spiritual world into which one ends up depends upon which fragment is separated. I had always separated soul-fragments that usually brought me into different etheric compartments, but seldom into astral compartments, and never into angelic areas.

Great was my amazement when I divided or separated the luciferic forces from the ahrimanic forces within my own chest. The threshold appeared and, in passing this threshold, I touched for the first time the angelic realms. It was like opening my heart to the angels. I had to ask myself why I had waited so many years to do this.

The two ways of separating Lucifer and Ahriman

If we study the statue 'The Representative of Man' by Rudolf Steiner and Edith Maryon (mentioned earlier as 'the Group'), we see that there are two Lucifers and two Ahrimans, thus making two sets of Ahriman/Lucifer pairs. As Lucifer and Ahriman often cooperate and work together, we have to see them as working in unison. One pair is shown with Lucifer above Christ and Ahriman below, and the other pair is situated in the horizontal, with Ahriman to the right of Christ and Lucifer to the left. The connecting lines go straight through the heart of the Christ figure.

I have 'experimented' with these two ways—horizontal and vertical—of separating the luciferic and the ahrimanic. It seems to me that the horizontal dividing brings forth the *angelic* realm, whilst the vertical dividing connects more with the *archangelic* realm—but as I am in the very beginning of this work, I cannot yet be sure.

Using the will and the Middle Point to fight the malevolent effects of electromagnetic radiation

It is possible to use the faculty of will to fight the adversaries created by both electricity and electromagnetic radiation. I will explain this in depth.

Electromagnetic radiation (EMR)
Electromagnetic radiation is energy transmitted in the form of electro-magnetic waves. The term is also used in part to denote the transmission

and propagation of such waves. Both visible light, radio waves, micro-waves and x-rays are examples of electromagnetic radiation.

The spiritual reality behind EMR

Like everything else in the created universe, the phenomenon of EMR consists of a *material* and a *spiritual* part:

- Particles and waves will be considered here as material, including the term 'energy', which is used by many in the New Age, alter-native, movements.
- The spiritual part is not the actual EMR itself, but the spirit beings that follow this radiation. These spirit beings are of an ahrimanic and luciferic nature, and form the spiritual background of electricity and magnetism.

Magnetism always creates demonic beings of a luciferic tendency, whereas the creation of electricity forms elementary beings of an ahri-manic nature. When we produce EMR via electricity, we also create luciferic elemental spirits because of the magnetic part of this radiation. Electricity is the fallen light ether and magnetism is the fallen chemical ether,* both of which can be categorized as subnature. These two divine ethers (light and chemical ether) have thus fallen into the powers of

---

* The teaching of the four ethers is essential within anthroposophy. In general, we can see these forces that act on human beings in the same way as the forces that act on the earth and the plants:

1. Warmth ether—this has a very active quality and is represented by fire as the physical element, which always needs something it can burn. This involves time, which is pro-gressing and has the quality of ripening. In the Human being, this is found in the *will*, in that if we are not doing something, the fire dies. Love enables the human being to be on fire, which is born out of our heart warmth.

2. Light ether—this represents polarities of darkness and light, with the physical element of air. This quality allows the distinction and makes visible boundaries of physical matter. It leads to the periphery and draws the viewer to feel as though he is being sucked into that periphery. This also gives the quality of levity where there is an elongation/uprightness and overcoming of gravity.

3. Sound ether/Tone ether—this exudes the quality of separation and connection. The physical element is water, which is connected to the Life ether and as such is recognized also as the Chemical ether. It is in this sphere that one experiences harmony, which is also related to all numbers and allows for analytical thinking.

4. Life ether is the great healer. This allows physical processes that have gone 'wild' to reintegrate themselves back into the life processes in order to create the balance of health again. This has the quality of integrating and uniting.

subnature and, as a result, 'malicious' elemental beings are created. There are different degrees of malevolence of these creatures, depending on whether the electricity is generated from:

- coal
- hydropower
- wind power (wind turbines)
- wave power
- solar power (solar panels).

The elementals created from these different sources look quite different and have different pathological and social effects. The worst and most pathological elemental beings are formed when solar panels are used in the production of electricity. This is also the most logical when we think that something as sacred as light is being pushed into the subnatural creation of electricity. It is like a double degradation of light.

Example 1

With the above knowledge of EMR, I did the following experiment. At a riding centre in Germany, there were fourteen horses, all of which were lame to different degrees. However, all of them had pain in the spleen area, between the sixteenth and eighteenth rib at the back, and this pain had then caused different types of lameness.

Just 100 metres from the stable there was a 4G phone-mast. The EMR radiation from this mast could be felt very strongly, and it was obvious to me that this was making the horses sick.

I had gathered a group of twelve people, and at a distance of approximately 50 metres, we all attempted to mentally push apart the forces of the adversaries abiding in the mast, and to thereby create a space for the Middle Point, the Christ-force. After 10 minutes, all pain in the back of the horses had gone, and within a few days all of them were free of lameness.

I checked the situation two years later and everything was still fine in this stable. The pathological aspect of the radiation was gone, although the mobile phones still functioned as usual. The malevolent spiritual forces were separated from the material EMR-radiation. This treatment was implemented by people who did not 'see' the spiritual elementary beings.

Example 2

A similar example relates to what I experienced in the United States in November 2018. I was sitting with some colleagues in a restaurant which had about twenty television sets, each showing their separate programmes. All those who were eating sat zombie-like in front of the sets, shovelling food into their mouths whilst their eyes were riveted deep into the flickering emissions.

I related the mast and horse experience in Germany to the three colleagues with whom I sat, and then proceeded to make the following experiment: Concentrating on one of the TVs, I separated the ahrimanic and luciferic powers, and almost immediately there was a significant change in the people who were watching this particular TV set. Suddenly, they became humanized, taking an interest in the food they put into their mouths, becoming alive in their movements, talking together and behaving in a clearly changed manner. My colleagues observed this change with astonishment.

An explanatory parallel from homeopathy

Homeopathic medicines are produced by separating the spiritual from the material, and one then uses the spiritual as a medicine for various diseases. This separation occurs by 'succussion' (rhythmic shaking) of the homeopathic remedies. Homeopaths remove the material part and let the spiritual remain. I do the opposite with EMR devices, by taking away the spiritual part and allowing the physical to remain.

The Middle Point of mechanical and electrical devices

This subject will probably be of vital importance in years to come. Today we all are under the most severe attack from electromagnetic radiation. This radiation comes from 4G-masts, 5G-masts, mobile phones and every kind of electro-magnetic device.

Since I discovered the Middle Point, I have for several years tried to find the equivalent within 'dead', manmade devices. Contrary to the belief that such devices are 'dead', as creations of the human mind they are endowed with a form of elemental life. They also contain the elemental forces of the luciferic and ahrimanic realms, without which material existence would not be possible. Although they are apparently inanimate machines, they also have the midpoint, the Christ Point, between the two forces.

I have tried, with 4G-masts, with TV-sets and with mobile phones, to concentrate my *will mind* on the Middle Point of these devices, to expand this Middle Point and thus weaken the adversarial forces. Over time, I have observed a marked effect on the allergic pathologies of the people and animals affected by this radiation. I would presume that this also goes for the insects in the natural world. Allergic, sensitive reactions to radiation and the resulting physical pain have completely disappeared after such a 'treatment' of only ten minutes. How can this be possible?

If we think about the making of homeopathic remedies, to a certain extent we split the physical substance from the spiritual remedy, thus using the spiritual part as the remedy without having to care about the toxic effects of the material substance. It is likewise possible to split the toxic part of radiation from electric devices; to split off the part that belongs to the adversaries, Lucifer and Ahriman, and to keep just the functional part—that of TV pictures, mobile phone conversations, electric cooking/warming, or those relating to any of the numerous other devices we use in our daily lives.

In such a partial splitting, we have to use our will mind. As described earlier, under 'splitting of our soul-fragments', we first lead our will down to the earth and then bring it up again. At the halfway point, it must be met by the intending thought, and in this meeting the force arises with which we can split the pathological from the physical, at least to such a degree that the pathological effect of the EMR is neutralized.

Travelling the East Coast of the USA: A road-trip from New York City to Florida

This very interesting road-trip became a study in etheric strength and ahrimanic power. Through this, I first became aware of the power of the adversaries that reside in the United States.

I was invited to the house of a person who claimed to have developed the ability to heal cancer with a specific intentional energy pattern, created by a unique form of meditation. This individual exclaimed further that the tumours they were treating first enlarged dramatically and later imploded. After this inflammatory reaction, the patient would be cured. I then asked the person if they could demonstrate this method on their dog.

Upon observing the technique being employed, I realized quite to my surprise that the etheric body of the pet was being taken backward in time to when its vital force was that of a younger dog. However, I also saw something else: before my spiritual eye, a circle of flames, accompanied by the sound of screams, emerged around the individual, as if the gates of hell had been opened. I am now convinced that assistance was being given from an adversarial force.

The next day, this dramatic encounter was followed by yet another spiritual experience. I was asked to give a lecture on anthroposophy in the community of Hawthorn Valley, NY. That evening, I discovered the unique features of the elementals living in this area. I watched them gather in a large group around the house where the anthroposophical meeting was held, and I somehow felt that they were longing for anthroposophy.

They looked very different from the elemental gnomes of my country, Norway. They actually appeared to be quite similar to the 'Bigfoot' in American folklore. They were naked and quite large, as well as hairy. Along with their large feet, they also had large eyes. In contrast, the Scandinavian gnomes are smaller, nicely-dressed and much friendlier.

The encounters continued. From the third to the seventh day, I was asked to teach a course in the Menla Mountains. An Icelandic woman called Bryndis Petursdottir was also invited to speak about her special ability to perceive nature elementals. In fact, she has a school in her native country where she teaches about the elves and hidden people that abound there. During her lecture, she stated that, even though she did not see Hidden People (as Icelanders call the elves) in these mountains, she met the guardians of the valley, described by her as a couple of huge etheric bears.

I also encountered these bears but, as I was trying to communicate with them, I realized that they detested the English language. This was so evident that they became somewhat aggressive when this language was spoken. I continued to try to communicate with them by using various other languages such as German, French, Spanish, Norwegian, and Danish. Finally, when I spoke Swedish, their demeanour changed and they began to respond.

Just like Bryndis Petursdottir, I had at first not been able to see Hidden People. However, a few days later, when I happened to look five to seven metres down into the earth, I finally saw them, and in large quantities! It was as if they were hiding from those of us living in the material world. Indeed, they are truly hidden.

Towards the end of the course, we visited a farm to diagnose and treat some horses. I immediately sensed that this particular farm was built at the same spot as an old Native American settlement. I also felt that the inhabitants of this settlement had been massacred. This reprehensible deed had left a very strong karmic ley line. I have discovered that the best way to remove a toxic ley line is to pray for forgiveness. When the class participants collectively prayed, the imbalances in the horses present in the barn immediately started to heal.

After the New York course was finished, it was then time to begin our journey by car to the centre of Florida to give yet another course. Accompanied by a friend, on the first day we travelled south to Virginia. While my colleague was driving, I felt a huge, dark etheric cloud impinge upon my etheric field, causing me some anxiety. I asked the driver if we were near the capital and she confirmed that indeed we were. In addition, I saw that this ahrimanic cloud seemed to stimulate the growth of all the local Bigfoots. I had a feeling that a strong ahrimanic entity was to incarnate soon in that area. I felt quite depressed by this thought, and this low mood remained within me for at least two days. In addition, I began to experience the presence of the Native American culture, and the massacres and killings that they suffered. I saw that these misdeeds were written in the etheric history of the entire East Coast.

The following day, we travelled further into North Carolina, to a place called Grandfather Mountain. This is a very special mountain, as it is inhabited by two trolls, one male and the other female. They were much stronger and more lively that their Norwegian equivalents.

We continued our North Carolina journey to a place called the Biltmore Estates. To my surprise, this was the farm and home of the Vanderbilt family. This is the family that, together with Rockefeller, has done more to destroy homeopathy in the USA than anyone else. In addition, they were the primary force behind the destructive aspects of capitalism. On this site, they have built a tourist centre complete with restaurants, expensive shops and a museum as a tribute to their legacy. The primary feature of this estate, however, is a looming castle on a large hill. This was the ostentatious residence of this family, and certainly symbolized their decadent lifestyle. I did not visit the interior of this building, as a large fee was required to enter its doors. This huge domain reminded me of the castle of Klingsor, and an equally huge demonic elemental hovered over the entire area. The whole place felt evil. I noticed a vast area of solar panels, constructed to supply electricity for this centre. I noticed more demonic elementals, which were created by this production of electricity from the divine light. They dominated the area around the solar panels.

We continued our journey into North Carolina, to visit Linville Falls, a natural wonder, considered one of the most beautiful sights in the Pisgah National Forest. The elementals in the waterfalls were also quite different from the Scandinavian water elementals. Like the earth elementals there, they were much stronger, wilder and quite naked.

We went to the pond below the waterfall, where several of the strongest elementals lived. In my pockets I had two stones from the Icelandic high elves. I decided to throw both stones into the repository under the waterfall, but immediately the elementals protested violently. They said that if I did such a thing, they would suffer pain for centuries. I then refrained from throwing these stones.

Amidst the sights and sounds of this part of the trip, I pondered as to why the Vikings travelled here to learn about these violent elemental-ahrimanic forces, and why their travels to America stopped around 1,000 AD. I also wondered why Americans often develop such strong and fundamentalist Christian beliefs. I think that both questions have the same answer. It appears that the Native American peoples understood the strength of these elementals and realized that if they could harness their dark force, they could then use it as a defensive weapon against marauders. From my observations, they seem to have developed the art of black magic to a high degree, as did the ancient Mexicans, according to Steiner. In the Mexican Mysteries, they developed the art of black magic to such a degree that they could almost have hindered the incarnation of Christ.

The Vikings also knew of the power found in the wilderness of North America and yearned to develop advances in both medicine and weaponry. They continued this search for almost a thousand years, until the dawn of the age of the intellectual soul. Viking initiates, and those in the high Church, understood that it would have been catastrophic to bring such knowledge of black magic into Europe. This same terrible fear of witchcraft by the Church also resulted in the atrocities of the witch-hunts, that were carried out a few centuries later. At a certain level, American Christians understood the destructive nature of such forces and, as a result, seeded a strong fundamentalist movement that has pervaded many parts of America to this day.

Passing the Mason-Dixon Line, the old borderline between the North and the South, presented me with a huge change in the elemental world—so I don't find it strange that this line is considered to be the border. South of this line, earth elementals get bigger and have a lighter skin. The air elementals have bigger wings and greater force. The etheric bodies of men and women living here are also slightly paler and 'thinner', which may explain the bestiality of many of the men living in this area. Reaching South Carolina, this impression became more prominent and clearer. We spent the night in the Deep South, close to the town of Mountain Rest and the Chattooga River, where the film *Deliverance* was filmed.

Travelling down the East Coast from north to south, I saw so much beauty and so much evil. It seems to me that these two things get along together very well. Travelling further south, we started to enter the land of slavery, into South Carolina and then Georgia. What interested me most in this area was that the trauma of the Native Americans changed to the trauma of the slaves, and possibly the Civil War. I saw this in terms of men in pain, but their etheric remains were quite 'white'. The elemental ahrimanic beings also became more and more 'white' the further south we went, and their appearance became more and more luciferic. Then, they started to have wings, looking almost like dragons. That was a feature of almost all the elementals this far south: they looked increasingly ahrimanic/luciferic. I also tried several times to talk with them in English. Every time they became angry and violent, and they grew in size. Swedish always seemed to be the language they liked best.

The next day we visited the slave market in Savannah in South Georgia. The only interesting thing to recount from this last part of the journey is that the painful silence of the etheric imprint of the slaves further north, in Alabama, changed to more of a 'crying' sound in Savannah, the centre of the slave market.

Farther south, in Florida, the elementals were more 'normal' and similar to the New York region, although the tendency to luciferic wings still remained.

Coming home to Norway one week later, I experienced a huge influence of the powers met and experienced in USA. There was a huge etheric hole in my chest that took me several days to fill and heal. It felt extremely depressing to live with this hole, but I recovered. After recovering, I felt so inspired by my experience with the tele-visions at the restaurant that I started to experiment more with the pos-sibility of 'separating' the toxic adversaries from the material part in electromagnetic devices. This will be described in a further book, already in preparation.

Chess and Christmas songs

Some of the stranger but very interesting discoveries that I have made— apart from solving the riddle of the five-elements and the changing effects of cancer treatment—are to do with:

- playing chess;
- walking in the forest; and
- singing Christmas songs.

Chess is becoming an increasingly important and popular game of strategy, capturing the interest and obsession of people of all ages and social classes. I have myself been an eager chess player for almost all my life, and still was until the day I discovered that Lucifer himself stood behind the five-element system used within acupuncture. In that very same moment that I realized the influence of Lucifer, I totally lost the ability to play chess. I started to defend my opponent's chessmen and not my own! The rules were, in a way, turned completely upside down. It was as if a completely new set of rules came into being, relating to caring for and supporting the opponent rather than winning.

That experience made me investigate more closely the effect of chess on the human soul. The results of this investigation showed that the thought structure used in chess is that which Ahriman prefers. The rigid rules—the fight to win, the joy when the other makes a mistake or overlooks a dangerous situation—are completely ahrimanic. This is what he thrives on.

Walking in the forest gave me a different experience after I realized why my cancer therapy had changed. This very interesting observation, relating to the change in my way of thinking, appeared simultaneously as I understood Lucifer's role in the development of the five-elements. The feeling of *knowing or not knowing where I am* has been completely reversed. When walking in the forest, I get a strong feeling that I *know* the places where I have *not* been before, but *do not* know places where I have walked many times.

This reversal of thinking may have similarities with my change in attitude to chess, where the 'concept of the enemy' was also completely reversed for me.

Christmas songs, and what they have become over the years, is an interesting study, and many will probably agree with my results. Most people today are in accord with the notion that Christmas has changed into a fiesta of commercialism, and that the original and true meaning of this day has disappeared totally—at least in our part of the world. According to Rudolf Steiner, the spirituality of a ritual, that originally was founded on true spiritual content, will totally change if the insight into the ritual has changed. If the understanding of a fundamentally sound and religious or spiritual ritual is lost or no longer understood, the ritual will attract demonic spirits, and to this effect the ritual will change from being beneficial to destructive.

I experienced this change in a particular 'heavy' way during Christmas 2018 when I was rehearsing for a church concert with my choir. One of the songs we were practising was a song called *It's Beginning to Look a Lot Like Christmas*, written by Meredith Willson. This is a song that hails the consumerism of Christmas, and states that, because of all the glitter and gifts, 'it's the most wonderful time of the year'. I went home determined to partake in that concert. The following two nights I had terrible experiences; I was haunted by ahrimanic spirits related to Christmas consumerism. Then I clearly understood that I was unable to partake in the planned concert.

5. Spiritual Training

Meditation

All training must contain an element of meditation. For me meditation is about *concentration* on a specific and limited *object* for a certain period of *time*. It always contains these three elements:

Concentration, which means that we must direct all our observation in the direction of the chosen object. It also means that we should not engage our thinking, feeling or will in this work. It is similar to when we separate our thinking, feeling and will (and possibly time), leaving only our 'I' consciousness. When I say that we 'direct our attention', it is this 'I' consciousness to which I refer. This attention (the 'I') can then be focused on whatever subject we want to investigate, and it can penetrate the object at three depths (see below).

A Focal Point, which means what we direct our attention to. It may be a physical object, a mental object like thinking or feeling itself, or it can also be 'time', such as an incident in the past. The object can also be penetrated in three depths or ways.

Time means that we should hold our concentration on the object for a certain length of time. The time aspect can also be held in three directions or depths.

These three 'depths', of both concentration, object and time, need to be dealt with in greater detail for clarification.

The three depths of *concentration* are:

- Staying with the consciousness, the 'I' outside the object: then we experience the object in imaginations or pictures (Imagination).
- With the 'I' entering the 'skin' or the outer layer of the object: then we understand what the object really is (Inspiration).
- With the 'I' going deeply into the object: then we feel that we enter into a deep communication with the object (Intuition).

The story below gives a sense of the difference between Imagination, Inspiration and Intuition.

In 1980, when I was training in acupuncture with the late Georg Bentze—who was a deeply spiritual Hungarian doctor—a bright halo appeared around his head. The halo was strong and intense, almost like a neon advertising sign. As stated before, the more important the message, the more physical the experience appears.

In this halo was written a date. This appearance of the halo with the date was the Imaginative *side of the experience. This I watched from outside.*

When I intensified my attention or concentration on the date and came closer to the 'neon' writing in my mind, I understood that this was his death date. This became clear and obvious. This was the Inspiratory *side of the experience.*

When I, with my 'I'-consciousness, then went 'into' the date, into the actual numbers, the presence of a dark entity appeared. The entity was death itself. This was the Intuitive *side of the experience.*

I told him that he only had eleven more months to live, to which he replied that I was the third person to tell him this.

He died exactly on that date, eleven months later.

The three depths of the *object* are described very well in the above example, and need no more description.

The three depths of *time* are actually the same as described earlier in relation to the three possibilities we have when we enter the streaming etheric between trees. Thus, we can go:

- *To the left* to enter the past. In this way we enter the past of this special object; it may be a tree, an animal or a physical object such as a knife or a gun.
- *To the right* to enter the future. Here we experience how the different future options may work out for any given individual.
- We can stay *in the middle* to:
  o Go out of time. Then time loses its importance and a 'nirvanic' consciousness appears. I consider this to be 'luciferic'.
  o Or, stay in the time. Then, a deep morally-inclined feeling of obligation to our own time and culture appears. I consider this to be 'Christian'.

Training the spiritual part of the twelve senses

As we have seen, we have twelve different sense organs or organ-systems through which we can perceive the physical world, the etheric world, the astral world and/or the spiritual world in their physical, divine or adversarial aspects.

The twelve senses have three levels of perception:

- The exterior level, relating to luciferic sense perceptions.
- The middle level, relating to the physical and spiritual perceptions.
- The interior level, relating to ahrimanic perceptions.

It is of crucial importance that we become conscious of these three different levels of perception, which are quite 'anatomical' and must therefore be understood as three different layers or depths of the physical sense organ:[*]

- We need to train in order to feel where, in our eyes, we perceive the luciferic observation of something that we *desire*. This place is in front of the eyes, 1-2 cm outside the cornea of the physical eyes.
- Then we move our attention to something that we have no desire for; to some indifferent physical object that is not important to us. We perceive this object in the physical part of the eye.
- Then we move our attention to something *living*, like a tree. We feel this perception in the spiritual part of the eye, which is at the same level as the physical eye (the good spiritual forces reveal themselves in the physical, not outside, as with the adversaries).
- Finally, we may look at our *mobile phone* and observe that our gaze will be activated somewhat behind the eyes, 1–2 cm deep.

This consciousness of perception is of crucial importance, and can be trained in all twelve senses, although I myself have only been able to train this differentiation regarding the eyes, ears and sense of smell.

Hearing is trained by switching between listening to the birds, the speech of friends, a loved one, the sound of the television or music played through a device.

We should also train to experience the difference between real live music (acoustic without amplification) and music heard through a microphone and amplifiers. This last example is often referred to as 'live' music. However, this is not the case. It is still ahrimanic.

I will now describe the training of the sense of smell in a more technical way.

As already explained, I have found, in my medical training, that there is a Middle Point in our bodies, where the healing force of the spiritual world resides. I call this middle point the *Christ Point*. About 60 per cent of people can 'smell' this point, but only 1% of all of my students are able to 'see' this point clairvoyantly.[†]

---

[*] This is described in detail in Addendum 1. I suggest you read this before you go further.
[†] See Rudolf Steiner, *Aspects of Human Evolution*, 8 lectures, Berlin, May-July 1917 (CW 176), especially lecture IV of 26 June.

The training of the sense of smell proceeds as follows: you breathe out and start to smell the upper part of the spine of your friend or patient. Then you move your nose relatively fast down the spine, all the way to the tailbone. When you reach the tail, the inhalation is finished. The whole spine is 'sniffed' in one inhalation. Around the heart area, the smell is quite different, within only a few centimetres. Most describe this smell as heavenly. Different words used are ambrosia, flowers, spring breeze and suchlike.

This is the smell of the spiritual healing force of Christ.

Training the dividing of thought from feeling and will

This training is of vital importance and you can do it when and wherever you like, in all situations of life. It is similar to active and conscious daydreaming, performed in a way in which you keep your feelings and will intact inside, but projecting your thinking outside. This sometimes happens involuntarily in boring lectures or conversations with people who do not interest you. Then, at a certain moment, your thoughts fade out into the vast expanses of the world (as this is usually unintentional, the thinking might be followed somewhat by the feeling and will, which should not happen if this is done voluntarily and fully consciously). In involuntary outflowing, the 'I' is also less present, but in conscious out-flowing, the 'I' must be fully present, even strengthened.

In the beginning, the novice may have problems in separating the thinking from the feeling, and the flowing out may be a combination of both thinking and feeling—the feeling being likened to a parasite of the thinking. In such a situation, we must further separate the thinking from the feeling by the conscious use of *directions*. We then consciously direct the outflowing of the thinking—together with the 'parasitic' feeling—upwards, not horizontally outwards. As the thinking is related to the upward direction, this will separate the thinking totally from the feeling.

In this way, we will reach the cosmic thoughts through the silver cord. This silver chord will then stretch from our third eye to the expelled thinking process. At this stage, it is no longer right to call one's thinking an *ability*, as we come to realize that it is not *our* ability; rather, it is cosmic thinking that we tap into. The remaining nucleus of thinking that stays within our head feels grey, stupid and uninteresting. This is *our* part of thinking.

In experiencing the cosmic thinking, we may feel *shame* regarding our own thinking—this thinking in which formerly we took so much pride.

With the expelled or divided thinking, you have the possibility of perceiving the cosmos in two ways:

- through an onlooker's perspective via the remaining thinking nucleus in your head;
- through the expelled part of the thinking.

These possibilities are described and dealt with under the sections on *Imagination*, *Inspiration* and *Intuition*.

Training the dividing of feeling from thinking and will

This training is much the same as described above, regarding the separation of thinking from feeling and will.

In separating *thinking*, we separate the thinking consciously from the head upwards, maintaining the silver cord connection between the third eye and the thoughts in a *vertical* direction.

Concerning the *feeling*, we will direct this soul property from the heart outwards in the *horizontal* direction, keeping the silver cord connection between the heart and the feelings. We then try to be conscious of the remaining part of the feeling found in our heart; and when we find this remaining nucleus, we try to contact the outer and outward projected feeling-part through the nucleus and the silver cord, consciously.

In the world we enter here, we will find the elemental world with all its different inhabitants. Entering into the feeling-elemental world with all our love is of great importance.

Training the dividing of will from thinking and feeling

This training is much the same as described regarding the separation of thinking and feeling from will.

In will, it is easier to separate this property from thinking and feeling than it is to separate thinking from feeling, as the will is considerably more different from thinking and feeling than thinking is from feeling.

In separating *will*, we separate this consciously from the limbs of the body downwards, maintaining the silver cord in the area of the lower abdomen, in a vertical direction downwards. Then we try to be conscious of the remaining part of the will found in the lower abdomen; and when finding this remaining nucleus, we try to contact the outer and outwardly projected part through the nucleus and the silver cord consciously.

At this stage, the forces of will that have been transposed into the earth may rise again at the command of our intention. They rise up as a stream of force that can be used beneficially, and must be met halfway with a stream of thought or intention directing the willpower to its goal, often via the arms or legs.

When entering the earth and elemental world, it is of paramount importance to muster good intentions and faith along with all the strength contained in the will.

Training to meet the Lesser Guardian of the Threshold

In my experience, meeting this Lesser Guardian of the Threshold is actually meeting *yourself*; in other words, to really see and accept your faults within thinking, feeling and will, in both the time-line and relating to karma. Training to meet these unpleasant creatures or entities requires *absolute honesty*.

In my opinion, the three animals described below are part of the Lesser Guardian.

Training to meet the Greater Guardian of the Threshold

This Greater Guardian of the Threshold is regarded by many as Christ in the etheric realm.

Meeting the Christ from my experience is twofold:

- Meeting the man, Master Jesus.
- Meeting the Christ in the form of Christ Consciousness.

There are many reports today about meeting *Jesus*, in stories and books. They describe this meeting as with a man who can show you yourself; a man who guides you, leads you and with whom you can talk. A companion that will be with you always, protecting and defending you.

With the possible exception of the very early and sparse beginnings I experienced in finding and treating the Christ Point, I have not yet met the *Christ Consciousness*, so I cannot expand on this subject as I do not have the experience.

Training to deal with the animals of the threshold

These animals are nothing but the outward projected faculties of your thinking, feeling, will and other soul-properties. Training to meet these animals without opening to the influences of the adversaries depends on cultivating *honesty* and *humility*. You have to come to the realization that your thoughts, feelings and will are not yours, and that you only tap into the vast cosmic forces of the Father God, the Son God and the Holy Spirit with their three feminine parallel forces of the Maria-Sophia, the Holy Daughter and the Holy Soul.

Training the passing of the threshold

The passing of the threshold is in a way much like dying. Throughout life, I have found several methods to train in this passing.

One quite effective and interesting method I used was in the local children's swimming pool in my town. This room was quite warm and under the water there were several lights dotted around the edge, just under the water line. I stood at a certain distance from these lights, contracting all my muscles, pretending that I was dying—at the border of death. Then I inhaled deeply, went under the water, pushed my body in the direction of the lights, and slowly breathed out. With my eyes open, I focused on the lights coming closer and closer. I pretended this was the dying process and that the lights were the light-filled tunnel on the other side of the threshold.

Another exercise was to build my own coffin. This coffin is kept it in my office where I see it every day. Each time I consciously become aware of my coffin, I slightly pass the threshold. The acceptance of death is the main training.

Training to see different aspects of the spiritual world

From my experience, I have realized that there are many different thresholds, and that the passing of these thresholds happens in a con-tinuous way. One way of experiencing this is to pass the threshold from different parts of the body and from different aspects of the soul. This means to part the thinking, feeling and will through *different parts of the body*, resulting in the fact that the expelled soul-forces pass through different thresholds and move to different parts of the spiritual world.

Training how to behave in the spiritual world

Only by entering the spiritual world in the right manner can such training be exercised. It is of crucial importance that your motive for wanting to enter the spiritual world is love and care for creation, all beings and God. If you enter out of egoistic reasons, or worse, with the intent to harm somebody, this will destroy all your future abilities and drive you into the darker aspects of this light-filled world.

Addendum 1

The Twelve Sense Organs and Their Developmental Significance

One of the most important concepts of anthroposophical literature is the influence of the Second Coming of Christ on assisting the spiritual evolution of the etheric cosmos and humanity. In order for us as material beings to observe such a phenomenon, it is imperative that we develop the spiritual aspects of our sensory organs to perceive the spiritual world. Several occultists have related this phenomenon to the activation of the chakras, especially the heart chakra. However, here I will focus on the development of our twelve spiritual sensory organs.

The reason why this development is so critical is that Christ will reveal himself again only in the etheric. Therefore, if we do not have the spiritual faculties to observe this profound event, it will pass unnoticed, resulting in consequences that will be catastrophic for all humanity. In addition, the adversarial forces will work diligently to thwart our efforts toward this necessary step in developing our spirituality.

Early in the year 1910, Rudolf Steiner spoke for the first time about the mystery of the true nature of the Second Coming. During this period, he gave a series of lectures on the subject, which he continued in subsequent years. He felt strongly about the importance of this theme. The study of the Second Coming of Christ, the collective threshold of humanity, and the opening of our spiritual sensory organs, is fundamental to our entire understanding of the meaning and purpose of the anthroposophical movement.

The first coming of Christ in the flesh occurred in an era in which human sensory organs could only observe material reality—at the deepest point of descent, in Kali Yuga or the Dark Age. Today, our spiritual senses are becoming more and more developed, and because of this, there is hope of experiencing Christ as he reappears in the etheric. At first, according to Steiner, he will be seen only by a few, but over the next 3,000 years, increasing numbers of people will develop the ability to see him.

Steiner said that in the future Christ would be felt or heard by those gathered to receive him. He described the extensive preparations made for Christ to be able to incarnate in the physical body of Jesus of Nazareth, especially in relation to Jeshu ben Pandira. In the two lectures given in

1911 on this subject,[*] he gave an explicit message to humanity about the importance of preparing for the Second Coming of Christ in the etheric. He added that the anthroposophical movement came into existence precisely for this purpose: 'All who work with anthroposophy and spiritual science must participate in the endeavours to evolve for Christ's Second Coming in eternity.'

According to Steiner, we have within us twelve sensory organs that are in continuous communication between our inner and outer world. Through these, human beings affect and are affected by the entire cosmos. In addition, from these sense organs we receive organizational and nutritional cosmic powers in order to build our etheric and spiritual body.

In the Old Testament, the twelve sensory organs were developed in Abraham and symbolized by the sons of Jacob. These sons represented each of the sensory organs, both as spiritual openings to the cosmos and as the zodiac power centres. In the story of Joseph and his brothers, we can see how these sensory organs were developed and then lost to humanity in our descent into matter. Within the story of the lost ten tribes of Israel, one can trace how these cosmic openings of the human being have been 'hidden' and yet have evolved differently in different parts of Europe. This explains the experience that many people, including myself, have that we experience things differently, depending on where we are in the world.

I would like to show how these sensory organs are formed as a response to the existing spiritual currents of the cosmos, as well as how new sensory organs form as a response to the ahrimanic, luciferic and azuric counterparts. These latter organs receive impulses and impressions to and from these entities, and this has been exacerbated by the emergence of the electronic age and poor lifestyles that result in diseases such as obesity. The development of doppelgänger organs darkens our ability to acknowledge the coming of Christ in the etheric realm.

The twelve sensory organs

Rudolf Steiner described these twelve organs as portals to both the physical, etheric and astral aspects of humans, as well as to the cosmos. Each sense is associated with an angel from the first hierarchy, and expressed in each of the twelve signs in the zodiac. In this way, they can be seen as a whole.

---

[*] *The Etherization of the Blood*, Basel, 1 October 1911.

Sense	Sense Level	Character	Sense-organs
1 Touch	Imagination	Cancer	skin
2 Life	Imagination	Leo	m. membranes
3 Motion	Imagination	Virgo	muscles
4 Balance	Imagination	Libra	inner ear
5 Smell	Inspiration	Scorpio	nose (memory)
6 Taste	Inspiration	Sagittarius	tongue
7 Sight	Inspiration	Capricorn	eye
8 Temp.	Inspiration	Aquarius	skin
9 Hearing	Intuition	Pisces	ear
10 Speech	Intuition	Aries	muscles and legs
11 Thought	Intuition	Taurus	ether body
12 'I' sense	Intuition	Gemini	skin

These twelve senses are shown in the Bible in the story of Joseph and his eleven brothers. In Genesis, Abraham (described as the first physically conscious man), miraculously had a son named Isaac, whose grandson was Jacob, who had twelve sons, of which the second youngest was Joseph. The story of Joseph is one of the most dramatic stories in the Old Testament. Joseph goes from being expelled from his brother's home in Canaan to becoming the most powerful man in Egypt. He is both wise, gifted and handsome, and these attributes bring him both misfortune and success.

The story begins with Joseph's dream, that someday in the future he would rule over his brothers. For this reason, along with the knowledge that Joseph was the favourite son of their father, his jealous siblings decided to murder him. When the attempted murder failed, he was sold as a slave to the house of Potiphar, the family of one of the Pharaoh's men. Eventually, in a twist of fate, he gained favour with the Egyptians and became the Pharaoh's right-hand man and supreme official of the kingdom. One of his greatest skills was the ability to interpret dreams, as a way to predict the future. Because of this special gift, Joseph helped Egypt escape a famine that devastated the rest of the region.

Over time, Joseph was reunited with his brothers, whom he forgave. Because of his forgiveness, his family was able to move to Egypt to escape the famine. Joseph's family was the foundation of the Israelites, and Egypt became their home, where they lived for many generations until Moses brought them back to the land of Canaan. The story of Joseph is not mentioned anywhere else in the Bible, but nevertheless it is the starting point for the rest of the Bible's history.

In a lecture, Rudolf Steiner discusses Abraham in the following paragraph:[*]

> On the occasion of my last visit here, we heard how in the end of the first millennium of Kali Yuga, man was given a kind of substitute for his loss of the vision of the spiritual worlds. This replacement was made possible through the fact that a particular individual, Abraham, chosen because of the special organization of his physical brain, was given a consciousness of the spiritual world without having the old clairvoyant abilities. That is why we, in the world of spiritual science, call the first millennium of Kali Yuga, 'Abraham's epoch'. This was the epoch when man truly lost direct vision into the spiritual world. However, unfolded in him was a divine consciousness that gradually penetrated into his ego, with the result of a heightened awareness of the divine related to human self-consciousness. In the first millennium of Kali Yuga, also called Abraham's epoch, the divine is revealed as the World-Ego.

Later in the lecture, he says:

> This Abraham epoch was followed by the epoch of Moses, when God Yahweh, the World-Eternal, was no longer revealed in the form of a mysterious guide of human destiny, as a god to a single people. In the epoch of Moses, this deity became apparent, as we know, in the burning bush, like the God of the Elements. And it was a big advance when Moses and the people through Moses learned the world-like godhead in such a way that they realized: the elements of manifested existence, all that are seen with physical eyes—lightning, thunder and so forth—are radiations, deeds of the world-I, ultimately of one world-I. However, we must clearly understand that this means a progression.

> Before the epoch of Abraham and before Kali Yuga, we find that, through the direct vision of the spiritual worlds made possible by the remains of ancient clarity, human beings saw the spiritual, as was the case in all ancient times. We have to go infinitely far back to find something else. People actually saw the spiritual in Dvapara Yuga, Treta Yuga, Krita Yuga. In other words, they saw it as a multitude of beings.

---

[*] *The True Nature of the Second Coming*, lecture 2, 6 March 1910.

You know that, as we step into the spiritual worlds, we find the beings of the spiritual hierarchy. They are, of course, under a unified guidance, but this was beyond conscious understanding in ancient times. The people saw the individual members of the hierarchies as a multitude of divine beings. Understanding them as a unity was only possible for the initiates. Now, humans can explore for the first time with their brain as their physical instrument. An ability had developed in a special way in Abraham, and this confronted him as he experienced the world-like manifestation in the different natural realms in the elements.

A further advance was made in the last millennium before Christ, in the Solomon era. Therefore, the three millennia before Christianity can be described by calling them by the name of the individual who shapes that epoch. From the beginning of the Kali Yuga to Abraham's era, man was prepared to recognize one God behind the manifestations of nature. First, Abraham's era appeared, then in the epoch of Moses, one God became the ruler of nature's manifestations. All this was intensified in the Solomon era when man was led through this last epoch to the point of evolution when the same divine being that was seen as Yahweh in the Abraham and Moses epochs took on a human form.

Thus, Abraham became the father of Isaac, who had a son, Jacob. God changed Jacob's name to 'Israel', which indicates that archangelic forces began to intervene. This intervention resulted in twelve sons being born. These twelve sons have since been related to the twelve animal images of the zodiac, and I wish to relate them to the twelve sensory organs, as shown in the table below.

Each of these twelve tribes lived in different areas of Israel. I have personally travelled throughout this country and have experienced that each of these sites is quite different. Emil Bock made the same observations in his books[*] about Christ's Life and the Old Testament. This is why Christ travelled throughout Palestine in a very distinct pattern and way with his disciples.

---

[*] *Childhood and Youth of Jesus* and *The Three Years*.

Sense level	Sense Organ	Zodiac	Body part	Jacob's son
Imagination	touch	Cancer	skin	Benjamin—LOST
Imagination	life	Leo	mucous membrane	Judah
Imagination	motion	Virgo	muscles	Naphtali—LOST
Imagination	orientation	Libra	inner ear	Dan—LOST
Inspiration	smell	Scorpio	nose	Simeon—LOST
Inspiration	taste	Sagittarius	taste	Gad—LOST
Inspiration	sight	Capricorn	eye	Reuben—LOST
Inspiration	temperature	Aquarius	skin	Zebulun—LOST
Intuition	hearing	Pisces	ear	Levi
Intuition	language	Aries	muscles/legs	Issachar—LOST
Intuition	thought	Taurus	brain	Asher—LOST
Intuition	'I' sense	Gemini	skin	Joseph (Ephraim and Manasseh)—LOST

The twelve senses in relation to the twelve sons of Jacob and thus the twelve tribes of Israel

The twelve tribes were divided into two parts: ten tribes founded the Kingdom of Israel in the north, and the tribes of Judah and Benjamin founded the Kingdom of Judah in the south.

The Assyrians and Babylonians invaded the northern kingdom and led ten of the Jewish tribes into captivity in Babylon, from which these tribes never returned. This led to the mystery of the ten lost tribes, which, according to tradition, have wandered to different parts of Europe and America. I find their migration to England and Ireland to be particularly interesting as, centuries later, Joseph of Arimathea brought the Holy Grail to these countries.

According to information from the American clairvoyant Edgar Cayce, groups of people from Palestine migrated particularly to Britain and America. That these migrations were important can be understood by recognizing that the entire earth has a holistic etheric force field, as described by James Lovelock. Rudolf Steiner also described the Earth as a living organism that acts upon the beings that wander around it. As human beings are organized and differentiated as to how their organs [including sense organs] are distributed over the body, so is the Earth also organized and differentiated with regard to the people who inhabit it. Therefore, it was very important that there was a diaspora of these ten tribes, or in other words, these ten moving sensory organs.

The senses of life and hearing were the senses that were not lost (the Israelites could still hear Yahweh, but not see him), and these remained in Palestine. The rest of the senses were spread throughout Europe, especially Britain, but also Scandinavia and America. Some of the Kabbalistic literature says that when the Messiah returns, these tribes will return to the Holy Land. In this way, the scattered parts of the remaining ten senses will be reactivated in those humans who are sufficiently spiritually awakened to become aware of the Second Coming of Christ. We are now living in that time.

However, just as the transcendental aspects of these twelve senses are about to open, which will result in the yet unaware humanity crossing the threshold en masse, so will a counterpower be strongly committed to preventing this.

This will happen in many ways, but I would like to elaborate on three methods:

1. Electronic communications media, including movies and TV (attack by both Lucifer and Ahriman).
2. Electronic music, meaning all music that has gone through an amplifier (attack by Lucifer).
3. The obesity epidemic that today we can see happening throughout the world (which obstructs both Imagination, Inspiration and Intuition, probably through an attack by Ahriman).

This book explains in detail how these oppositional forces, especially Ahriman, will proceed to manipulate and inspire the modern evolution of electronic technology in order to assume control of humanity. In addition, the technology and lifestyle that has led to the obesity epidemic will be a contributing factor. Ahriman's main area of attack are the portals of the sense organs of the eyes, ears and skin.

The threefold, fourfold and twelvefold human

Steiner categorized humanity's physical and supersensible sheaths variously as either threefold, fourfold, sevenfold or ninefold. From one perspective, he divides human beings into four layers, consisting of physical body, etheric body, astral body and 'I'. However, this fourfold being can be described from a different viewpoint as having either seven or nine levels, with the higher levels being called Budhi, Manas and Atma.

At its core, a primary trinity of the dominant soul forces of thinking, feeling and will governs our higher self, as well as the whole of Creation. They represent the basic processes by which our entire cosmos is organized and developed. Everything that exists is reflected holographically in all aspects of creation. This trinity encompasses the entire cosmos, the divine angelic hierarchies, as well as the sub-nature of spiritual beings such as elves, hidden people and other elemental beings. This latter aspect of our universe can be seen with the spiritual eye as an upside-down reality (or it may be our world that is upside down!). In this way, one can imagine that the soles of our feet are touching their feet, and that their world is a reverse image of our cosmos.

Some would say that the explosion we have seen in electronics and communications represents humanity's finest hour. With a simple stroke of a key, we can find information about almost everything. We can get in touch with anything and everyone within seconds, and this has changed our perception of the written word. In fact, language has now unwittingly become an effective weapon against our fellow man. With this in mind, it is no wonder that the existence of electronic technology has created an effective and powerful tool for the adversarial forces.

The three cosmic forces play a role in all aspects of our lives. They are extensively described in the anthroposophical medical system as the three basic poles:

- nervous and mental system (thinking);
- rhythmic system (feeling);
- metabolic/muscular/skeletal system (will).

However, it is crucial that we understand that we can also apply this template to the twelve senses, especially when considering the steps toward spiritual initiation:

- Imagination (the four physical senses of touch, life, movement and orientation);
- Inspiration (the four soulful senses of smell, taste, temperature and vision); and
- Intuition (the four spiritual senses of hearing, speech, thought, and sense of perception of the 'I' in others).

The senses as described by Steiner are extremely complex formations, as they show both an outward and inward direction of flow. For example, the eyes that perceive the cosmos send an outward flow of ether so that they can also receive an inbound flow of information from what they are looking at. It is a general spiritual rule that any movement automatically creates a counter-movement. This law also includes time (the two opposite time streams). The energy that flows through the sensory organs, builds up the entire body (apart from the head, which is organized according to the forces of the Earth).

Rudolf Steiner says in his *Agriculture Course* on 16 June 1924:

Now all that is present as substances in the head organization is composed of earthly matter. (So it is also in humans, but let us limit ourselves to the animal now.) Any substance found in the head is earthly substance/matter. Already in the embryo life, earthly matter is steered into the head organization. The entire embryonic organization is arranged so that the head receives its substance/matter/material from the ground. There we have earthly substance.

On the other hand, all that we have as substance/matter in meta-bolism and limb organization, such as this substance, penetrates our bones, limbs, muscles, bones, etc.—it does not come from the ground at all. It is cosmic substance. It comes from what is absorbed by the air and the heat found in the atmosphere around and above the ground. This is important. You must not consider a claw or a hoof as if it was formed by the physical substance that the animal eats in one way or another and then finds its way into the hoof and is deposited there. That is not true at all. In fact, cosmic matter is absorbed through the senses and breath. The animal eater has the sole purpose of developing its inner forces of movement, so that the cosmic principles can be driven all the way down to the metabolism, all the way into the limbs, hooves and claws. The cosmic substance penetrates these parts, but here it is only cosmic substance.

Exactly the opposite applies to the forces that lie behind the head. In the head—as far as the senses are mainly stationed there, and the senses perceive the cosmos—we have cosmic powers; while in the system of metabolism and limbs we are dealing with earthly forces—cosmic substances and earthly forces. (As for the latter, just remember how we move; we constantly place ourselves in the earth's gravity, and in the same way, all that we do with our limbs is related to the earthly.) The twelve sensory organs are developed in the physical/material body, and as such, they have their spiritual counterpart in the physical (blueprint), the etheric and the astral body.

Subnature	Sense organ	Power type	Body part	Time epoch with maximal activity
Elemental (E.) world 1	touch	electric	under/over skin	540–720
E. world 1	life	electric	front/back mucous membrane	720–900
E. world 1	motion	electric	front/back muscles	900–1080
E. world 1	orientation	electric	front/back inner ear and eye	1080–1260
E. world 2	smell	magnet	outside/ inside nose	1260–1440
E. world 2	taste	magnet	outside/ inside tongue	1440–1620
E. world 2	sight	magnet	outside/ inside eye	1620–1800
E. world 2	temperature	magnet	outside/ inside skin	1800–1980
E. world 3	hearing	nuclear power	below ear	1980–2160
E. world 3	language	nuclear power	muscles and legs	0–180
E. world 3	thought	nuclear power	under etheric body	180–360
E. world 3	'I' sense of others	nuclear power	out/in skin	360–540

The twelve senses as mirrored in the sub-earthly (elemental) dimensions

We can say that:

- In the physical body the sensory organs tell us about the physical world.

- In the physical body's blueprint (where we can also find the 'I'-organization), the construction of the sensory organs can be used not only by our own consciousness and intuitive sense of clarity, but also by the azuras.
- In the etheric body, we can find the sensory organs that can be used by our imagination, by our etheric body, by our intellectual soul, but also by the ahrimanic beings.
- In our astral body, we can find the sensory organs that can be used by our intuitive clairvoyance, our soul body, the emotional soul, but also by the luciferic beings.

The part of the twelve senses that can be used by the counter-powers of the luciferic, the ahrimanic and the azuric forces, is in close relation to our doppelgängers in a unique way.

- The human or 'karmic' doppelgänger uses the physical sensory organ as used in the material world.
- The ahrimanic and luciferic doppelgängers (and the online doppelgänger, which I suppose is related to the azuras), create their own 'spiritual' parts of the spiritual sense organs:
  - The ahrimanic sense organ is formed from between one and two cms deep inside the material body, although this varies individually.
  - The luciferic counterpart of the sense organ is more superficial than the organic/material organ, as it is formed in the astral body. It can be as much as ten cms outside the physical body.
  - The azuric sensory organ I can see as a kind of perimeter around the physical body. It is much more difficult to see than the other three (physical, etheric and astral).

For example, with regard to the eye, the ahrimanic sense organ is about one cm behind the body's material eye structure, while the luciferic one is about ten cms in front of the eye. With my clairvoyant ability, I perceive the ahrimanic structure as greyish, resembling a tin plate, as described by Hans Christian Andersen in *The Tinderbox*. In Ibsen's *Peer Gynt*, one can find an interesting reference to such an eye. A form of surgery is even described where a gap can be cut in the eye in order to 'change' the appearance of the opposing forces and make us believe that everything we see is beautiful (in this example, to assure the Troll King that a marriage between Peer and the sorcerer's ugly daughter is possible).

Looking at electronic displays also activates and develops these structures. If one considers all twelve sense organs, the fact that all these senses are also used by three doppelgängers, and that each organ is involved in both an outgoing and an ingoing stream, we can conclude that there are 72 qualities that must be considered when understanding sensory function. Note that all twelve senses can create spiritual observation in all parts of the cosmos, in the etheric, the astral and the spiritual, related to thinking, feeling and will. For example, if the spiritual eye is developed in the etheric field, we refer to the ability as clairvoyance.

Sight
The first sensory organ I will discuss is the eye, which is the basis of the visual ability and fundamental to the faculty of Imagination and clairvoyance. When seeing through the physical eye, I have observed that when one looks at a living object, especially in nature, the angels in the higher spiritual hierarchies also share this observation. I have also observed that the sensory organs with little fat, such as the eye and the ear, have a stronger affinity for the etheric and thus the imaginative.

In contrast, when staring at a mobile phone screen, the observations are made deeper in the body; they lose their colours, they become dead and ahrimanic, and the humanness disappears from them. I have also observed that when someone watches pornographic images on a mobile phone, an eye is formed that is approximately 8–10 cms in front of the physical eye, i.e. the luciferic eye, located in our astral body.

From my viewpoint, if we observe the results of the outgoing stream of ahrimanic and luciferic forces on the underlying nature of the physical world and then on the virtual electronic world, I think both demons can thrive in the online world, including the internet, artificial light, LED displays, computer monitors and cell phones. Because of this, I consider handwriting to be a safer method of communication, as it is under the domain of the angels.

The strength of these doppelgängers is woven into sensory observations. Paul Emberson argues[*] that the use of computers stimulates the power of the forces of opposition, enabling them to grasp more strongly our existence. For example, if you watch a movie, this will actually reinforce the visual feelings of the ahrimanic doppelgänger, which is deeper in the body than the physical organ; or, if we see 'astral movies' (something we often do today) it will strengthen the luciferic sense organ, which lies in the astral body outside the physical body. As mentioned above, this astral eye is grey and large, resembling a tin plate.

[*] This is described in Paul Emberson's *From Gondishapur to Silicon Valley*.

In 1917, Steiner addressed his concern to his audience about going to the cinema. He describes the eyes of those who watch films as 'taking on' the senses of Ahriman. It seems to me that, through their doppelgängers and through the proliferation of electronic media, the ahrimanic and luciferic forces are becoming more and more sophisticated.

The healthy spiritual forces, by contrast, avoid such devices that create a substitute online community instead of healthy social connections among people. An even more sinister connotation lies in the increasing inability to promote our goal of spiritual initiation through the process of Imagination, Inspiration and Intuition. Therefore, we should try to limit electronic communication in our daily lives by minimizing the use of email, Facebook and other forms of social media. Our soul life, our eternal life and our physical bodies depend on our limiting this use.

We must now protect our future for ourselves, our children and for the spiritual future of humanity. Just as Goethe wrote that the sun creates our human eyes, likewise, the existence of virtual media and electronic devices will create the need and lay the foundation for an ahrimanic eye.

Hearing

In today's society, we meet electronic music in all places, at all times and in all forms. Hearing as a transient sense is also one of the two senses that in ancient times remained in Israel. Attacks by the opposing powers via hearing are amongst the oldest forms of attack. These began with the discovery of the phonograph, invented by Edison in 1877, which led eventually to long playing records (vinyl) and compact discs. In this technology, the voice is disconnected from its original ethereal relation to the larynx, the creative part of man, which in the future will be so significant in our evolution.

When I observe people who listen to music that has been reproduced via a disc or via amplifiers, I see that they 'hear' with an 'ear' that is 10 cms from the physical ear, in other words, in their astral body. This is a typical luciferic ear, which links this musical experience to those powers and avoids the connection to the good spiritual world, the world of the angels.

In Sandefjord, Norway, I once attended a chamber concert with voice and piano. I thought this would be without amplifiers, but it was not. I observed the ears of the listeners, and although the music was of prime quality, it was mostly in the luciferic ear that the activity was happening. I find little enjoyment in going to concerts anymore.

Feeling

The third sense organ I will discuss here is the sense of touch. This has elements of touch, temperature and 'I' senses. The physically related organ that is associated with these senses, the skin, is interestingly divided into three layers: epidermis, dermis/corium and subcutaneous.

It is important in this context to note that the skin is the active sensory organ of all three senses mentioned above:

Level of sensing	Sense and relation	Zodiacal sign	Physical body part
1. Physical (Imagination)	sense of touch	Cancer	the Skin (epidermis?)
8. Mental (Inspiration)	sense of temperature	Aquarius	the Skin (dermis?)
12. Spiritual (Intuition)	sense of others, the 'I'	Gemini	the Skin (subcutis?)

We should keep in mind that Steiner emphasized that the good powers of the future will come from the Pisces–Virgo axis (Morning–Evening Power). The adversarial powers use forces from the Gemini–Sagittarius axis. The midday forces that flow into Gemini can be abused by the occult fraternities in the West, and the midnight forces from Sagittarius can be abused by the occult fraternities in the East. I sense that, in the highest spiritual dimension, a transfer of this sense of touch to the ahrimanic forces will lead them to utilize the forces that come from Gemini and which are related to the skin. Perhaps that is why Joseph left the dominion over this sense to his sons?

Below are my own early observations in connection with the skin, or the three skin senses (the skin in its three shades, related to Imagination, Inspiration and Intuition, to touch, temperature sense and the 'I'-sense), from back when I started at the veterinary school in Oslo, before I had even heard of Steiner or anthroposophy.

In the first years of my studies, I spent some time between lectures watching tourists, especially those who were overweight (at that time, mostly Americans, but today the majority of people). I saw with my spiritual eye that in many of these people the skin, especially around men's stomachs, was stretched in such a way that the physical layer of fat was outside the normal ether body. The fat tissue was detached, loosely hanging out of the ether body.

In this way, the effect of the skin as an emotional organ in terms of spiritual sensing (which allows for, among other things, clairvoyance) was reduced. In other words, obesity can have a debilitating effect on all the three abilities expressed in Imagination (touch sense), Inspiration (temperature sense) and Intuition ('I'-sense). Therefore, when a person is on a weight reduction programme (diet), they may be able to better develop their spiritual feelings, since their etheric body may eventually be aligned with the skin, or even go beyond the skin (which is a necessity for the development of real clairvoyance). Being slim thus reduces Ahriman and Lucifer's deleterious effect on this particular emotional organ.

This may be why Christ fasted when he resisted the temptations of these demonic powers during his 40 days in the desert. Being thinner allowed him possibly to achieve a higher level of spirituality (not that He needed it, but as a picture for humanity to follow).

To understand how obesity can affect spirituality, we must look again into the skin's relation to the etheric body and the spiritual blueprint of the body. We must then understand how Rudolf Steiner described clairvoyance as a relationship between the physical body, etheric body and astral body, especially when the spiritual bodies extend beyond the physical form. For example, the etheric body of the Atlantean period was outside the physical/material body, especially in the region of the head. In this way, Atlanteans were clairvoyant and thus able to observe the etheric world, but not consciously, as we do today. However, if the etheric body is within the boundaries of the physical body, supersensible vision is greatly reduced.

It seems to me that the ahrimanic and luciferic sensory organs have developed both in line with our growing love of technology (especially over the last 20 years), and with the growing epidemic of obesity throughout the world today. This epidemic is perhaps the greatest danger to our spiritual development, and the opposition forces[*] have cunningly linked the addiction and desire for sugar and food to the same dopamine system that heroin is associated with. This modern disease of civilization, obesity, will thereby be able partly to remove Imagination, Inspiration and Intuition from our spiritual potential and surrender these potential abilities into the claws of the opposition forces.

---

[*] These forces of opposition have some control over the nervous and glandular systems, especially in the production of hexagonal structures and 'reward' substances such as dopamine (see Addendum 2 on hexagonal structures).

Addendum 2

The Mystery of the Hexagon

The pineal gland and hexagonal structures—The incarnation of spiritual entities

In several sculptures throughout the world, we can see a structure looking like a pine cone. We can find this structure even in the Vatican (see photo). But this is no usual pine cone, but a detailed and exact sculpture of the so-called 'pineal gland', as this has an external similarity to the pine cone.

A statue of the pineal gland in the Vatican

This gland is also called the epiphysis.* It produces, among other substances, melatonin, a substance that is excreted during sleep. The observant reader will see the molecular structure, especially the combination of a hexagonal and a pentagonal structure, their interrelation and the placement of the nitrogen atom (N) in relation to them.

---

* The pineal gland carries signals from the eye. In the epiphysis, this leads to inhibition of the excretion of melatonin. The philosopher René Descartes thought that this gland was the meeting place of soul and body. In some primitive creatures, this gland is still a physical eye. The gland is also stimulated in an unknown way by some drugs, such as DMT.

Melatonin

Molecular structure of DMT

Some scientists claim that DMT[*] is produced in the pineal gland, but how much and why is uncertain. People who have taken this drug have surprisingly similar visions and experiences.

The pineal gland is twofold:

- a part related to the blood circulation as an endocrine gland;
- a part related to the nervous system, although it is not directly attached to this system. This part consists of nerve cells derived from the hypothalamus.

The neural part of the pineal gland seems to be quite isolated from the rest of the body. This indicates a very interesting schism. We know from Rudolf Steiner that the nervous system is especially closely related to the adversaries (especially the ahrimanic doppelgänger) and is totally void of the human 'I'-organization. This part of the pineal gland has an especially close relation to the hexagonal structures, especially melatonin. According to Rudolf Steiner, this gland is a remnant of the 'third eye', an organ that was active in our clairvoyant ancestors—especially in Atlantis—by means of which they could see the spiritual world.[†]

In this section, I will try to show that the hexagonal structures—both in the microcosm of molecular structures and in the macrocosm of structures built by insects or in stone formations—either have a close connection to, or even are, portals between the physical and the spiritual. Spiritual entities—both the good and the not so good, and including our own spiritual sheaths—are able to travel through these portals. The luciferic

---

[*] Dimethyltryptamine is one of the most potent and discussed hallucinogenic substances known at present time. See: https://www.youtube.com/watch?v=6umdf4Ef970

[†] 'Later [in world development] the rest of this light-filled body expands beyond the still open head, and creates the first primitive earthly sense organs. This first seed of the eye, which was at that time looking like a polyp, was an organ that could sense the warmth streams, both close and further away. In this way, this organ is both material and clairvoyant. The individual experienced a sense of distant streams of warmth in Imaginations. It was then as such still not a physical eye, but a spiritual eye. Man had at that time only a dreamlike and imaginative picture-consciousness. The last remnant of this once so light-emerging structure is today the pineal gland.' Rudolf Steiner, *Universe, Earth and Man*, Lecture VII.

adversaries especially can use them, but when the hexagonal structures crystallize, the ahrimanic ones can too.[*]

One of the more important of these hexagonal structures we will consider, is the benzene ring. I will later describe in what interesting way this structure was discovered within chemistry.

In this connection, we must remember that what we call the adversarial powers, whether luciferic, ahrimanic or azuric, are forces or entities we need in our human development. Without the snake in paradise (Lucifer) we would not have been able to incarnate and obtain freewill, and without the entity we today call Ahriman, we would not be able to master the hardness of the material world. It is only when these adversarial forces get too strong or unbalanced that they really become adversarial.

Benzene Ring

During sleep our astral body—the upper, cranial part—is outside the physical body. We are then open and ready to be influenced by impulses from the spiritual world. Here, I will try to show that the presence of hexagonal structures will facilitate this stream of cosmic information.

In relation to this, it is of great interest that during sleep the pineal gland is active, excreting the hexagonal substance melatonin. In my view, these hexagonal structures open specific portals to the spiritual world, to cosmic entities from both the good realms of angels and unfortunately also to the adversaries, both luciferic and ahrimanic spirits.

In structures influenced by the ahrimanic forces or entities, which are, as we now know, sclerotizing and mineralizing, we will expect that this presence in the pineal gland will cause mineralization. We see this clearly in the pineal gland, where often 'brain sand' is found,[†] a phenomenon we

---

[*] Ahrimanic forces or demons, and of course Ahriman himself, will try to make the spiritual development of the human race materialistic. They will sclerotize the body and take away the spiritual experiences of man. They are especially related to electricity. Luciferic forces, and of course Lucifer himself, will try to make the spiritual development of the human race too otherworldly in an attempt to make humans forget their earthly mission. They are especially related to magnetism, and like the ahrimanic spirits, they want to lead man away from his godly destiny and necessary development.

For a deeper and more comprehensive description and discussion of these subjects, I refer the reader to the general anthroposophical literature, and also to my book *Demons and Healing*.

[†] Brain sand, *acervuli cerebri*, is the term used for calcium salts in the pineal gland, which may be seen in x-ray pictures of the brain. They appear as a normal change of age and have not been seen as a problem for the function of the gland itself. Similar crystals have been seen in other places of the brain, especially in *plexus choroideus*, where the cerebrospinal fluid is produced. The cerebrospinal fluid is, according to Seiner, also of great importance to the function of our spiritual bodies, especially in remembering.

often see in elderly people. According to Rudolf Steiner,[*] this brain sand, this dead and mineral substance, is actually the specific place of incarnation in the material realm of the spiritual, of the 'I'. We understand then that we really need the ahrimanic adversaries to incarnate in the material realm of existence.

The brain sand itself forms hexagonal structures as it crystallizes, and opens a portal to the spiritual world, letting the 'I' incarnate. Between the single crystals, a weak electric current is created (piezoelectricity), expressing the presence of ahrimanic forces, and these crystals and electric current can actually function as a receiver of radio waves (see Paul Emberson's *From Gondishapur to Silicon Valley* and the writings of Professor Gerald Pollack).

As a veterinarian, agronomist and producer of medicines (which I always test on myself), over many years I have marvelled at the hidden relationship between molecular structures and the effect they have on the human (and animal) etheric body and astral body. Certain substances open the way for ahrimanic entities, some for luciferic, and still others open for greater parts of the spiritual world, although never the whole, as the spiritual world consists of very many aspects.

In a very interesting lecture[†] about specific aspects of medical plants and homeopathic and anthroposophical medicine, Steiner describes a special effect we can observe in the spiritual constitution of a person after ingesting an extract of belladonna. He states that this influence will stay in the etheric/astral configuration for a long time. I became very interested when I studied Steiner's drawing of the influence of belladonna on man's spiritual sheaths, especially in the region of the stomach, and compared this drawing to the molecular structure of atropine. Atropine is the active part that carries both the healing and the destructive forces in belladonna and is a key substance in this discussion, as it contains both pentagonal and hexagonal structures in its molecular construction.

If we compare Steiner's drawing of the spiritual structures appearing in the stomach region (where he clearly draws both pentagonal and hexagonal structures), it has a remarkable similarity to the molecular structure of Atropine, especially on the right side of the person's stomach region. I believe that this cannot be pure chance.

---

[*] Rudolf Steiner, *Harmony of the Creative Word*, GA 230, lecture 6.
[†] *The Driving Force of Spiritual Powers in World History* (Steiner Book Centre, Toronto 1972), GA 222, Dornach, 22 March 1923.

Rudolf Steiner's Blackboard Drawing on the Effects of Belladonna

Fish toxins

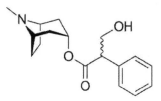

Molecular Structure of Atropine

There has been a recent article in *Psychedelic Press*[*] on the relationship between Christianity and the shared experiences from ingesting the hallucinogen ciguatoxin, produced by the fish *Sarpa salpa*. The author implies that the Christian doctrine may have emerged as the result of specific hallucinations brought about by such a toxin.

Although I certainly do not agree with Memfer's conclusion that the *origin* of Christianity comes from this molecule, I do believe that under the influence of psychotropic agents, one may experience the reality of these concepts. There may also be insights that can be gleaned from the investigation of the relationship between the molecular structure of such compounds and religious experiences. Furthermore, it may prove fruitful to discuss whether such experiences might be real or just 'hallucinatory',

---

[*] 'CTX: An early Christian entheogen?'—Memfer (pseudonym), *Psychedelic Press*: volume XX, 2017.

and which areas of the spiritual world are actually opened using these molecules.

Memfer argues that the iconic symbol of a fish—the representation of Christ in early Christianity—is perhaps more related to the hallucinogenic experience induced by the ingestion of toxic fish such as Sarpa. As further evidence, the author presents narratives of two subjective experiences using this toxin.

The first case is a 40-year-old man who became ill two hours after ingesting fresh-baked Sarpa. His symptoms were nausea, followed by blurred vision, muscle weakness and vomiting. He further discovered that he was unable to drive due to the distraction produced by the sound of 'screaming animals'. The effects of the fish toxin wore off after 36 hours.

The second subject, a 90-year-old man, also experienced hallucinations, but of screaming humans and squawking birds. In addition, for two nights he had horrifying nightmares. Fortunately, after a few days, the effects of the fish toxin subsided.

Although I strongly disagree with the conclusions drawn in the article, it nevertheless illustrates how hexagonal structures can mimic fundamental religious experiences and feelings. We must remember here that the luciferic powers are very good imitators of these feelings and experiences. When reading carefully about the actual experiences of the two patients, I have some difficulties in accepting these as religious experiences; they seem to me to be demonic in nature.

This underlines my assumption that various hexagonal structures based on the benzene ring occur in all mind-altering substances, and that these substances can open portals in the astral and etheric bodies to the spiritual world, via the twelve senses described by Rudolf Steiner.

Hallucinogenic experience: reality or fantasy?

The first premise of this addendum requires the reader to assume that the experiences induced by the use of psychedelic substances may indeed open a portal to an 'alternate reality'. In addition, this reality is the dimension referred to in anthroposophy as the 'spiritual world'.

The second premise relates to the theory that the hexagonal structure of the benzene ring found in the majority of mind-altering chemical compounds may act as the bridge between these two oppositional realities.

The final premise requires a deeper understanding of the teachings of Rudolf Steiner, which imply that the spirit world contains both benevolent and harmful domains. For the observer, the ability to discern the difference between these domains can often be problematic.

Anthroposophy (spiritual science) and the teachings of Rudolf Steiner

In order to accept the above premises, it is of paramount importance that the reader has a basic understanding of the tenets of the anthroposophical body of work. In his first, more philosophically-oriented phase, Steiner attempted to find a synthesis between science and spirituality. His philosophical work from these years, which he termed 'spiritual science', sought to apply the clarity of thinking characteristic of Western philosophy to spiritual questions, differentiating this approach from what he considered to be vague approaches to mysticism.

In the second phase, beginning around 1907, he began working collaboratively in a variety of artistic media, including drama, the art of movement (developing a new artistic form, eurythmy) and architecture, culminating in the building of the Goetheanum, a cultural centre to house all the activities of anthroposophy. In the third phase of his work, beginning after World War I, Steiner worked to establish various practical endeavours, including Waldorf education, biodynamic agriculture and anthroposophical medicine.

Steiner advocated a form of ethical individualism, to which he later brought a more explicitly spiritual approach. He based his epistemology on Goethe's worldview, in which 'thinking ... is no more and no less an organ of perception than the eye or ear. Just as the eye perceives colours and the ear sounds, so thinking perceives ideas.' A consistent thread that runs from his earliest philosophical phase through his later spiritual orientation is the goal of demonstrating that there are no essential limits to human knowledge.

In 1899, Steiner experienced what he described as a life-transforming inner encounter with the being of Christ. Previously, he had little relation to Christianity in any form. Then and thereafter, his relationship to Christianity remained entirely founded upon personal experience, and was thus both non-denominational and strikingly different from conventional religious forms. Steiner was then 38-years-of-age, and the experience of meeting the Christ occurred after a tremendous inner struggle. To use Steiner's own words, ' ... the experience culminated in my standing in the spiritual presence of the Mystery of Golgotha in a most profound and solemn festival of knowledge'.

The encounter with spiritual beings while under the Influence of hallucinogens

Anecdotal reports have described that, whilst experiencing drug-induced hallucinations, individuals have experienced encounters with 'extra-terrestrial' entities. This could be one of the reasons why some believe that such entities are mere hallucinations rather than real and living beings of the spiritual world. However, it is my experience that psychotropic substances can open doorways or portals into a *real* spiritual world. This doorway, once opened, can be travelled both ways, thus allowing both good and bad entities living in the spiritual world to invade the physical body, and for the user of such substances, in turn, to enter the spiritual realm.

Therefore, I believe that if one makes the decision to ingest such substances, he/she needs to be conscious enough to protect oneself against such alien influences—which under the influence of any drug is extremely difficult to do. According to anthroposophy, it is of paramount importance to keep our higher consciousness, or our 'I', free of such entities in order to protect our overall health.

According to Rudolf Steiner, the benevolent entities (angelic beings) that have our wellbeing at heart, want us to develop as spiritual beings. This is in stark contrast to the entities connected to the ancient 'holy' plants referred to in the Bible. While the good spirits wait for our con-scious invitation in order to appear, beings belonging to the darker forces do not need such an invitation, and this can lead to possession. Therefore, in order to be clear about who and what it is we are dealing with, we must understand this spiritual dimension, know its inhabitants, and be able to protect ourselves should we meet such undesirable influences.

In summary, Rudolf Steiner believed that to accomplish this protection one must understand how to balance the adversarial powers (Lucifer and Ahriman) using the Christ Consciousness.

When I was a student at the Norwegian School of Veterinary Science, the professor in pharmacology told us about all the effects of the natural and synthetic substances that contained the benzene ring, especially when this ring was in close proximity to a nitrogen molecule, with two or three carbon molecules in between. This, he told us, would result in the most potent hallucinogenic substances.

Saint Anthony's Fire

In medieval times, a disease unexplained for centuries was Saint Antho-ny's Fire. This disease could kill whole villages, and up to 1800 AD, several altar paintings were made to heal or lessen the symptoms of this terrible disease. Today we know its cause is a toxic fungus that grows on wheat and rye. Its Norwegian name, *meldrøye* (meaning a way to make the flour last longer), had its origin in the fact that people looked upon the black-coloured substance growing on the grains as a welcome way to extend the available food, especially during years of poor harvests. My father told me that when people died from eating this black corn, there would be more flour for the survivors! Maybe this was just his black humour . . .

This black fungus produces a very toxic and lethal substance called ergotamine, that contains several types of hexagonally-structured molecules, and some of these are almost identical to what today is known as LSD. Those who ingested grains containing this fungus suffered sudden and severe cramps and heat flushes that could be so strong that it felt like fire going through the body. After the cramps came hallucinations. People ran around screaming in the streets and fields, and many threw themselves into rivers or wells to lessen the symptoms. Most died from cramps in the breathing system or the heart, often after a long and painful development of the disease. From old journals, we know that 40,000 people died in Southern France in the year 994 from this poison. The last time such an epidemic occurred in Europe was in 1951. This happened in the small French town of Pont St. Esprit, where only four people died.[*]

As mentioned earlier, LSD was found to be based on the described secale alkaloid, and the hallucinations related to a so-called 'bad trip' may well resemble many of the secale hallucinations.[†] While still at the veterinary school, I thought that this hexagonal structure of the benzene ring was really an artificial portal to the spiritual world, especially to the domains of Lucifer and Ahriman.

---

[*] Usually, people looked upon diseases as a punishment from God, and from this belief the word 'hellfire' originated—*ignis sacer* (holy fire)—as an explanation for the burning feeling they felt in the body. The church let people believe that, even if they themselves knew the cause of the disease, and prescribed praying and other clerical exercises as a remedy against the symptoms. In 1093, a special monastic order was instigated to deal with the disease, and inside the walls of the monasteries, grains were harvested and carefully freed from all infected fungus. In that way, people never doubted that the prayers and sacrifices and money had helped, and did not suspect the diet given them by the monks. As the patron for this order of monks was St Anthony, it was named the Order of Saint Anthony.

[†] The fungal infection of grains is caused by *Claviceps purpurea*. This fungus produces many types of alkaloids, among others, ergotamine and ergotoline. These alkaloids are used as medication, especially within gynaecology and migraine treatment.

Ergotamin, a Sekale Alkaloid from the Fungus

For a person who has taken a dose of DMT, and describes what he experiences, these descriptions correlate very closely with the descriptions Rudolf Steiner has given of the Eighth Sphere.* This sphere is in the spiritual dimension—at least for the time being it is spiritual—but later it will become material to such an extent that it becomes indestructible. This is where Ahriman is building up his future kingdom. In this sphere, there are strange creatures, often insect-like, and the whole structure of the place is built over hexagonal structures.

Some people, especially those interested in New Age spirituality and who use DMT as a consciousness-opener to the spiritual realm (DMT is the active ingredient also in Ayuahuascha), believe that they really have entered the spiritual world, where they can talk with aliens and insect-shaped nature spirits. They can find these insect-shaped beings very intelligent, and do not realize the immense intelligence of Ahriman.

---

* What is the Eighth Sphere? To understand this expression, we have to understand that it is not a particularly well-known realm or a greatly understood concept among people with spiritual interests. For those who know, the concept is quite frightening. It is the sphere where all ahrimanic deeds, thoughts and concepts materialize in a separate physical planet. In the far future, this planet will be left behind by the common development of the universe and humanity. It is where deeds done without soul or consciousness will end up. In my opinion, this is also where all our experiences with synthetic drugs, synthetic additives, pharmaceutical medicines and artificial food will take us. Also, I believe our work and preoccupation within the field of computer technology (machines without soul), discussions on Facebook, conversations through email, and all lifeless computer interactions where the soul cannot enter, will end up in the Eighth Sphere. Many occultists have spoken and written about this sphere, but there has been much disagreement and discussion about what it is, where it is and how it is organized. Some think it is connected to our present moon, whilst some believe it to be 'sub-earthly'.

Rudolf Steiner gave lectures on this subject in the following volumes: *The Occult Movement in the Nineteenth Century*, lectures 4 and 5, October 1915, Dornach, GA 254; and *Foundations of Esotericism*, lectures 14 and 18, Berlin, October 1905, GA93a. In these lectures Steiner says that the Eighth Sphere belongs to our physical Earth. We are surrounded everywhere by Imaginations into which the aim is that mineral materiality shall continually be drawn. Its substance is far denser than the other mineralized substances. Its density is of a far denser physical-mineral character than exists anywhere on the earth. Hence, Lucifer and Ahriman cannot dissolve it away into their world of Imaginations. This sphere circles around as a globe of dense matter, solid and indestructible.

Rudolf Steiner had the strong conviction that it was very dangerous to enter the spiritual world without adequate preparations and the necessary ability to separate thinking, feeling and will, as well as opened spiritual sense organs. When entering the spiritual world, it is also important to know that we have to balance the adversarial forces, the ahrimanic and the luciferic powers. This can only be done by understanding and working with the Christ. To understand this concept properly, it is important to get to know what Rudolf Steiner has told us about the spiritual world, and that this world contains entities that are both necessary and sometimes harmful. This question of balance is just as true in all other areas of life, from foodstuffs to work or relaxation.

Relationship of Carbon, Nitrogen and Oxygen

Hallucinogenic chemical effect on the human body
As a student of veterinary medicine, I remember learning about the existence of these benzene rings. I also learned that substances containing a nitrogen atom followed by two or three carbon atoms and a benzene ring, are present in most hallucinogenic substances. Therefore, I hypothesized that this hexagonal shape may provide a link to other-dimensional qualities.

Depicted above are the molecular structures of some of the more important psychotropic substances used today. For example, psilocybin (5-MeO-DMT) is a hallucinogenic compound that is similar to chemicals produced in the neurogenic part of the pituitary gland. The most common psychedelic drug, LSD, has a similar chemical composition.

5-MeO-DMT is a substance that is produced in several of our organs, in the nervous system and as such in the nervous part of the pineal gland too. It also is found in several plants. According to Rudolf Steiner, the nervous system, and therefore the nervous component of the pineal gland, belongs to the spiritual heights, including the spheres of the adversaries. There is speculation as to whether this substance is released in great amounts at death.

Ahriman's trap

I have asked myself the question if this hypothesis about 5-MeO-DMT might be right, and if this substance accounts for the 'near-death experiences' written about in many books. I am inclined to think that if it is true that at death this substance is released from the nervous system—a system that is under the control of the adversaries, especially the ahrimanic powers—then this may be their last attempt to open the portal to the Eighth Sphere. This is the very place where Ahriman wants to lure human beings and, by doing so, wrestle them away from their God-destined necessary development, which in anthroposophical literature is described as the evolution from Saturn to Vulcan.

Rudolf Steiner talks about atomic structure further in the third lecture of the *Agriculture Course*. The following is a direct quote from this discussion:

> But we must now go farther. I have placed two things side by side; on the one hand the carbon framework, wherein are manifested the workings of the highest spiritual essence that is accessible to us on Earth: the human ego, or the cosmic spiritual being which is working in the plants.
>
> Observe the human process: we have the breathing before us—the living oxygen as it occurs inside the human being, the living oxygen carrying the ether. And in the background, we have the carbon-framework, which in the human being is in perpetual movement. These two must come together. The oxygen must somehow find its way along the paths mapped out by the framework. Wherever any line, or the like, is drawn by the carbon—by the spirit of the carbon—whether in man or anywhere in nature, there the ethereal oxygen-principle must somehow find its way. It must find access to the spiritual carbon-principle. How does it do so? Where is the mediator in this process?
>
> The mediator is none other than nitrogen. Nitrogen guides the life into the form or configuration, which is embodied in the carbon. Wherever nitrogen occurs, its task is to mediate between the life and the spiritual essence, which to begin with is in the carbon-nature. Everywhere—in the animal kingdom, in the plant and even in the Earth—the bridge between carbon and oxygen is built by nitrogen. And the spirituality which once again with the help of sulphur is working thus in nitrogen, is that which we are wont to describe as the

astral. It is the astral spirituality in the human astral body. It is the astral spirituality in the Earth's environment. For as you know, there too the astral is working—in the life of plants and animals, and so on. Thus, spiritually speaking we have the astral placed between oxygen and carbon, and this astral impresses itself upon the physical by making use of nitrogen.

Nitrogen enables it to work physically. Wherever nitrogen is, thither the astral extends. The ethereal principle of life would flow away everywhere like a cloud, it would take no account of the carbon-framework were it not for nitrogen. Nitrogen has an immense power of attraction for the carbon-framework. Wherever the lines are traced and the paths mapped out in carbon, thither nitrogen carries oxygen—thither the astral in the nitrogen drags the ethereal.

Nitrogen is forever dragging the living to the spiritual principle. Therefore, in man, nitrogen is so essential to the life of the soul. For the soul itself is the mediator between the spirit and the mere principle of life. Truly, this nitrogen is a most wonderful thing. If we could trace its paths in the human organism, we should perceive in it once more a complete human being. This 'nitrogen-man' actually exists. If we could peel him out of the body, he would be the finest ghost you could imagine. For the nitrogen-man imitates to perfection whatever is there in the solid human framework, while on the other hand it flows perpetually into the element of life.

In order to understand the effect these compounds have on how the individual perceives the spiritual world, we need to understand its inhabitants. As mentioned above, Steiner divided the malevolent forces into two fundamental archetypes. He often referred to these forces as 'demons'.

He calls the first archetype Lucifer. The entities representing this impulse are usually very beautiful, attractive and often female in appearance. They are described throughout history and in many religious manuscripts. In Tantric Buddhism, they are often considered benign, and they help people to acquire knowledge and artistic inspiration. In the *Tibetan Book of the Dead*, they are described as helping deceased spirits. Lucifer means 'the light bearer', and as such, these beings emanate a strong blinding light. Although seemingly spiritual, they can often lead one astray.

Folklore describes this confusion immediately after death. The soul is presented with two lights to follow toward the afterlife. One light is bright and blinding, the other soft and subtle. Most are tempted to choose the brighter, luciferic light. However, the better choice is to follow the soft light, the one that leads to Christ, the only path that will lead to salvation. When the *Tibetan Book of the Dead* was written, Christ had not yet appeared, therefore the luciferic influence was the only one that could help with mankind's spiritual evolution.

Therefore, I suggest that hexagonal structures provide not only an opening to the spiritual world, but also that specific compounds provide access to specific aspects of this domain. For example, regions controlled by luciferic influences are illuminated by the effect of LSD, DMT or Psilocybin. This is especially true for DMT, which is produced by the pituitary gland, the remnant of our sixth chakra or third eye.

According to Rudolf Steiner's descriptions of the Eighth Sphere, it is a world inhabited by insect-like beings. In my experience, it can be entered by the ingestion of DMT. In this world, the inhabitants appear insect-like. This becomes even more significant when one considers the hexagonal structure of the insect eye. In addition, insects tend to construct hexagons, such as the honeycomb. From my studies in anthroposophy, I have concluded that it may also be the final depot for those of us who fall prey to a soul-less attraction for the lifeless and artificial, such as synthetic drugs, additives, pharmaceutical medicines and artificial food.

Other lures include our preoccupation with the field of computer technology, a world of soul-less and life-less machines. This also includes those who mindlessly partake in functions requiring the use of computers, such as discussions on Facebook, conversations through e-mail and all lifeless computer interactions, where the soul can neither enter nor participate. The consequences regarding the abuse of technology are ominous. Many occultists have spoken and written about the Eighth Sphere, with many variations and even more conflicting theories as to what and where it is and how it is organized. As we have seen, Rudolf Steiner had his own opinions and gave several lectures that mentioned the Eighth Sphere.

Some studies have shown that at the moment of death, the pituitary gland excretes a large amount of DMT. This fact may provide an explanation to the importance of the excretion of this substance at such a significant time. If one agrees that DMT is capable of opening a portal to the luciferic world, this would explain the near-death experience of seeing a bright light. Although a possible source of comfort, as stated earlier, the brightest light presents the path toward Lucifer.

The potential dangers of entering the spiritual world by taking different substances without sufficient preparation

A fundamental teaching within anthroposophy is the meeting of the Guardian of the Threshold. This guardian stops you from passing the threshold and entering the spiritual world without a certain preparation. You have to understand and control your thinking, feeling and will, as these three soul forces separate when entering the spiritual world. They do not function as they have been functioning here in the physical world. If you are not trained in dealing with the single soul forces you will lose the control you need in the spiritual world.

Rudolf Steiner described these three soul forces, and the parts of them that one has not mastered, as three animals:

- One crooked, bluish, skeletonized animal that represents the mistakes and faults in your will.
- One ugly and lying, yellowish creature that represents the mistakes and faults in your feeling.
- One sneering, reddish creature with bared teeth that represents the faults and errors in your thinking.

Steiner says that these animals can also be perceived as:

- A dragon (The Door of the Sun) in the will.
- A huge lion (The Door of the Elements) in the feeling.
- A flying head with wings (The Door of Death) in the thinking.

The Vikings knew about the existence of these three animals or soul forces that had to be acknowledged and transformed before you could reach the spiritual world in safety. They described the way over to the spiritual world as a bridge, *Hjallarbrui*, and on this bridge there were three animals that hindered you in passing:

- A bull that was trying to head-butt you—this happened when you had not mastered or prepared sufficiently the will.
- A snake that was trying to bite you—this happened when you had not mastered or prepared sufficiently the feeling.
- A dog that was trying to bite you—this happened when you had not mastered or prepared sufficiently the thinking.

Steiner then tells us what will happen if you bypass these animals without the proper strength or preparation, for example, by using drugs and other hexagonal-structured substances.

In a lecture on 2 March 1915,[*] he says:

> Opposing this, there is the inclination of most people to enter the spiritual world by a more comfortable way than through true meditation. Thus it is possible, for example, to avoid the Gate of Death, and, if the inner predisposition is favourable, to approach the second portal. One can reach this through giving oneself up to a particular image, an especially fervent image which speaks about dissolving oneself in the Universal All and the like, recommended in good faith by certain pseudo-mystics. By this means, the exertions of thinking are stupefied and the emotions are stimulated. The emotions are whipped into fiery enthusiasm. By this means one can, to begin with, certainly be admitted to the second portal and be given over to the forces of will, but one does not master the lion; one is devoured by the lion and the lion does with one what it likes. This means that fundamentally occult things are taking place, but in essence they are egoistic. That is why it is constantly necessary—although one might say it is also risky from the point of view of true esotericism today—not to make a reference to a mysticism that simply whips up the feelings and emotions. This appeal to what stimulates a person inwardly, whipping him out of his physical body but leaving him still connected with the forces of the blood and the heart, the physical forces of the blood and the heart, does undoubtedly bring about a kind of perception of the spiritual world which may also have much good in it; but it causes him to grope about insecurely in the spiritual world, and renders him incapable of distinguishing between egotism and altruism.

This means that if we skip preparing ourselves through getting to know our feelings, our thinking and our will, we are not able to experience the spiritual or the good forces but instead will be misled down pathways of illusion by the adversaries.

The hexagon's relationship to membranes

Another interesting aspect of hexagonal structures can be found in the research of Professor Gerald Pollack.[†] He discovered that when water is placed close to a membrane, a fourth phase (distinct from solid, liquid and gas) appears as a sort of gel. This additional phase assumes a hexagonal

---

[*] *Esoteric Development*, lecture 10, 'The Three Decisions on the Path of Imaginative Cognition: Loneliness, Fear, Dread'.

[†] See Pollack, Gerald, *The Fourth Phase of Water*, Ebner and Sons, 2013. He is best known for his controversial work with the fourth phase of water.

structure. He also found that this unique water compound is capable of producing an electric current from sunlight. From this research, work is presently underway to invent a 'water battery'.

Through my own research, I have found that spiritual beings are attracted to membranes or interfaces, and the hexagonal form of the gel-like fourth phase of water opens a portal to specific adversarial spiritual beings. The more malevolent ahrimanic beings are attracted by electricity. Therefore, the 'water battery' may have greater implications than simply providing an inexpensive source of power.

The discovery of the benzene ring

How this structure was discovered yields interesting information about its possible luciferic origin. Lucifer can sometimes appear as a type of dragon. In relation to this, Friedrich August Kekulé (the German chemist who

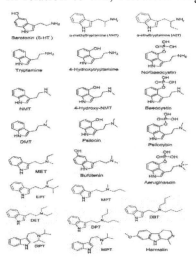

Some hallucinogenic substances

discovered the benzene ring) wrote about two dreams he had at key moments of his work.

In his first dream, in 1865, he saw atoms dance around and link to one another. He woke up and immediately began to sketch what he had seen. Later, he had another dream in which he saw these atoms form themselves into strings that moved about in a snake-like fashion. This vision continued until the train of atoms formed into an image of a snake eating its own tail. This dream gave Kekulé the idea of the cyclic and hexagonal structure of benzene.

Examples of hexagonal portals in nature

An interesting example of the connection between hexagonal structures, luciferic beings and hallucinogenic properties is Fingal's Cave in Scotland.* (The same hexagonal structures can be found at the Giant's

---

* 'On the isolated island of Staffa, near Iona in the Inner Hebrides of Scotland, an extraordinary collection of stalactites compressed by the surging water creates not only a cathedral-like space inside a cave but also perpetual sound, as the wind and water ebb and

Contd.

Causeway, Country Antrim, Northern Ireland.) Some say that Fingal's Cave was used for Druidic initiations. Later, it became famous as the source of inspiration for Mendelssohn. In my opinion, Mendelssohn was influenced by the opening of a luciferic portal related to the time of the year—the type of light that was illuminating the cave at the moment of his inspiration—and the hexagonal structures of this landmark.

A Scottish writer, Iain Thornber, has suggested a new link between Mendelssohn's *Hebrides Overture* and this landmark. Mendelssohn visited the cave in 1829 while on a tour of Scotland, and completed his *Hebrides Overture* on 16 December 1830, the only day of the year the cave is fully illuminated by sunlight, which Thornber thinks is no coincidence. Although he couldn't have seen this for himself, the boatmen could well have told him about it. It has often been reported that one can hear music whilst visiting this cave. I have personally experienced this music and was transposed into another realm of existence.

flow. This place is called Fingal's Cave—a source of mystery, spiritual insight and artistic inspiration for centuries. Mendelssohn and Turner were fascinated by it. Esoteric philosopher and educationalist Rudolf Steiner thought that Fingal—the chief of the ancient Celts, who preserved their religion and culture against pagan marauders—was the great pre-Christian initiate. The cave looms large in the fragmentary poems of Ossian, collected by the eighteenth century poet James Macpherson. The poems, subject of controversy even to this day, were a great influence on Enlightenment and Romantic figures as diverse as Thomas Jefferson, Walt Whitman, James Fennimore Cooper, Dickens and many others.' From *Fingal's Cave, the Poems of Ossian and Celtic Christianity* by Paul Marshall Allen, Joan deRis Allen, Continuum 1999.

An important question in this connection is whether the spiritual music heard in this cave is coming from the beneficent forces or the adversarial ones. The true spiritual world was in olden times called the home of the 'music of the spheres', but this world can be copied and distorted by the luciferic forces, as can many other phenomena, though in a beautiful way.

Hexagonal structures in the insect world: the beehive

We cannot deal with hexagonal structures and their effect on humans without considering the insect world in general, and bees in particular. First, we have to consider how the insect world relates spiritually to the rest of the world, especially the human world. Insects, spiders and crabs (especially insects), are characterized by a division of the organism into sharply defined parts. The respiration is highly developed.

In insects, there is a very clear distinction between the three main parts of the body—head, thorax and abdomen. The legs are attached to the middle part, the thorax, and there are always three pairs (hence their name *hexapoda*). The skin is transformed into a hard sheath of chitin, a substance very near to cellulose in its composition. Cellulose is the substance from which the cell walls are made in plants, and the relationship between the cell wall and the chitinous sheath is one of many, appearing between the two kingdoms in this group.

There are four separate stages in growth. This animal metamorphosis consists in the development from the egg, to the larva or grub, then to the cocoon, and finally to the perfect insect. As with worms, with insects everything is divided into parts. This may be seen further in the formation of colonies, where every individual insect is separate from the others, but from the functional point of view they form a unity. Everything is divided up in this group—the body in space, the development in time, and the colonies in organization. There are also innumerable species, so that even in this direction the division is manifold.

There are innumerable connections between insects and the plant kingdom. As Rudolf Steiner has discovered, the metamorphosis of insects has a deep connection with plant growth. The plant develops from the seed to the leaf-bearing stage, the bud stage, and finally the blossom. As Goethe has indicated in detail, these stages are interchanging contractions and expansions. In the insect there are also four stages, but each stage arises as a metamorphosis of the previous one and is independent of it, evens as regards locomotion.

There is a deep inner connection between insects and plants. The

140   EXPERIENCES FROM THE THRESHOLD

insects are really a repetition of the flowering plants in the animal kingdom. The mutual correspondence between insects and plants, as for
example those between butterflies and bees on the one hand and blossoms
on the other, can easily be understood when we know that the blossom is
a butterfly which has no locomotion, and the butterfly is a flying blossom.

This theory will also explain mimicry. That locust, which is called 'the
walking leaf', does not take the shape of a leaf because it imitates the leaf,
but such locusts have the inner structure of the leaves they appear to copy.
An inner relation between the two organisms concerned must explain all
mimicry.

This will explain the strong relation between the insects and hexagonal
structures such as the beehive, and also the effect of honey or bee-poison
on animals or human beings. The very life and spiritual origin of insects
tell the story of belonging to the luciferic realm of existence.

Honey also works in human bodies to counteract the sclerotizing
ahrimanic forces, which are today stronger that the luciferic ones. In this
connection, we must remember that, as human beings, we really need
both the ahrimanic and the luciferic forces, but we have to keep them in
balance. In olden times, the luciferic forces tended to take the upper hand,
but today the ahrimanic forces are overwhelming. We need to strengthen
the luciferic forces over the ahrimanic forces, but above all, the cosmic
force that is situated between the two, that keeps both in balance, and that
is the Christ force.

A spiritual investigation of the fire ant in Florida

In late autumn 2018, I stayed for some weeks in Middle Florida, giving
some courses there. One day I happened to step into a nest of fire ants,
and they gave me multiple bites. They have a special toxin that causes skin
eruptions the next day—at least this is what happened to me. With my
ability to view the spiritual world, I observed these fire ant eruptions
clairvoyantly, and immediately I could see into the Eighth Sphere, the
same sphere that one may perceive after taking DMT. This suggests
strongly to me that insects, at least the poisonous ones, are related to this
Eighth Sphere.

Conclusion

It is my hope that the reader will be inspired to investigate the theories
presented in this addendum regarding hexagonal structures and the
existence of the reality of a spiritual dimension. I believe that although

accessing these portals can transport us to other dimensions, it can also take us to situations where we can encounter malevolent entities. This is especially true when utilizing hallucinogens as a shortcut to entering these worlds.

Therefore, I implore the reader to research alternative methodology such as spiritual meditation, as suggested by the teachings of anthroposophy. In my opinion, this is truly the only way to use the gift of being able to visit these dimensions for our true purpose, which is to evolve as spiritual beings and to be a part of the global transformation of mankind in the service of all that is good.

A note from the publisher

For more than a quarter of a century, **Temple Lodge Publishing** has made available new thought, ideas and research in the field of spiritual science.

Anthroposophy, as founded by Rudolf Steiner (1861-1925), is commonly known today through its practical applications, principally in education (Steiner-Waldorf schools) and agriculture (biodynamic food and wine). But behind this outer activity stands the core discipline of spiritual science, which continues to be developed and updated. True science can never be static and anthroposophy is living knowledge.

Our list features some of the best contemporary spiritual-scientific work available today, as well as introductory titles. So, visit us online at **www.templelodge.com** and join our emailing list for news on new titles.

If you feel like supporting our work, you can do so by buying our books or making a direct donation (we are a non-profit/ charitable organisation).

office@templelodge.com

TEMPLE LODGE

For the finest books of Science and Spirit